Reflections

Reflections

Steve Summers

To order additional copies of this book, contact:
Xlibris
1-888-795-4274
www.Xlibris.com
Orders@Xlibris.com
805867

Contents

A Day of Days

Today marks a day I'll forever hold next to my heart. It would have been my dad's eighty-eighth birthday. I still and will always talk with him. October of this year was a bittersweet month. Our anniversary was October 1, then on the tenth mine and Wayne Newsome's birthday. Lost Wayne to a tragic car wreck forty years ago, and on the thirtieth, the day of Dad's death in 1990, I talked with him and asked if I should write a story of him. He answered back, "No, please have a good day and enjoy your day outside doing something to ease your pain and let it go," and I did. This may sound far-fetched for some, yet it is the truth. I will always talk to him, backing up to the day I learned of his death.

On a beautiful autumn day as I parked my truck at our old home place out in the country, Sherry was standing on the front porch. It was October 30, 1990. She said she needed to talk with me. As I approached Sherry, I saw a look in her eyes I'd never seen before. She told me to sit down, and then she told me of Dad being gone. Then and there I fell completely apart. Later that evening Susan, Carl, and I gathered together to discuss making the trip to West Virginia. It was so sudden—his death. Only the three of us made the trip home the following day on a flight out of Dallas to West Virginia. We had a small layover in Atlanta. There I saw a paper from Georgia. I told Carl I should buy this for Dad, he loved to read, without thinking why we were going. I put it back and walked on.

Not a word was said on the plane ride to West Virginia. I sat with my sunglasses on in utter silence, keeping my eyes hidden from the tears that flowed down my face. Arriving in Charleston, Tom and Mae were there to carry us to Kopperston. Once again I sat in silence.

Seemed a lifetime for the ride to Mom's. Once getting to Mom's, the house was full of family. As I stepped in the kitchen, I turned and walked back outside to try and put myself together. Didn't work. So I stayed outside, until my cousin Billy came out to see about me, finally making my way back into our little Kopperston home to see Mom.

She seemed better than anyone there. I know now she was only being strong for her children. My dear sister Sarah was only twenty-three years old and took care of almost all the details and arrangements the night of Dad's viewing at Evans Funeral Home. It was packed. I stood alone, until seeing an old friend. She offered her condolences. We talked for a short time. The next day was his funeral at Toneda Baptist Church. As I exited the car on the steps of the church, Jess Brunty was standing there, a welcoming sight for me. Sherry and I lived on Crouch's farm in a trailer that Jess owned. This was our first place to call home. A day later, a trip to Rockwood, Tennessee, to lay Dad to rest.

I thank Billy more than he'll ever know. I rode to Tennessee with him, a six-hour drive. He helped me so much. My love for him for being who he is, is indescribable.

Two days later we flew back to our homes and tried to get on with our lives, a journey for me that still hurts twenty-four years later.

One last thing to add. When Mom and Dad were here in 1989 on miners' vacation, Dad and me planned a trip to Corpus Christi to go deep-sea fishing. We both loved fishing and had never been salt water fishing. I told him in a year I would have a new engine in my old truck and a thousand dollars saved for us to go. He passed before the trip was taken.

A year later my brother Carl came to see me on the one-year anniversary of Dad's passing. As Carl drove up, I was so happy to see him. I started to cry. So did he. I remember exactly what I said to Carl: "I have a new engine and a thousand dollars but no dad to go with."

This story I dedicate to everyone who has lost a parent or even both.

A Christmas Story

This is a story that had gotten lost as well.

January 6, 2016, 5:27 p.m.

A Christmas story.

At Purzackley, one minute and thirty-two seconds after Thanksgiving, I was sitting in my recliner, sucking the last bit of turkey off the bone, and watching football, fixing to take a nap. My bride, Sherry Summers, interrupted me and said, "Hey, let's get the Christmas stuff out of the attic." I'm like "I don't think so" to myself, yet I did to make all bright in the Summers' casa, pissing and moaning to myself once again. So we did. Then I got my trusty blankie and slobber cloth, fell fast asleep in my recliner for a couple of hours.

As I awoke, there she was decorating with a wild look on her face like this has to be done now. So I bounced from wall to wall still half asleep to lose some ice tea that had built up in my bladder like a raging bull wanting out. I think I hit the toilet. I cleaned my bathroom anyhoot, so what's the difference. I'll get it Monday or one day soon. As the years passed, Sherry bought a lot of pretties for our home, most of them running off electricity. As I make my way back to my recliner and sit down, the TV goes off, I thinkin' it's time for the next game. Then it dawns on me. The breakers have tripped from her pretties. Now it's time to turn a slew of them off.

I reset the breakers. The game is already on, not happy once more—we discuss what can be plugged in and what can't. A semi-agreement is reached, I thought. How wrong was I. Real wrong.

As the days pass and Christmas gets closer, it's a losing battle for Steve—I very seldom win. Let me rephrase that—I never win. Two days before Christmas I'm so mad I'm half blind with anger and wanting to squeeze the life from her veins. Instead I play it cool, fetch my good old baseball bat. Outside I go and start beating the electric meter from the brick—finally falling to the ground. Mission accomplished. Go back into our home and the power is still on and my TV is off once again—shaking my head of straw.

A new approach is what I need. Out to my shop for a long-handle ax. And yes it's cold and muddy. Forgetting my flip-flops, the mud is squishing between my toes. the closer I get to the electric meter, the madder I get. Now ready to chop the wires into. My first swing got them both about a minute later.

I land in an dairy pasture around thousands of cows around me when I woke up one hour later approximately four miles from our home on Farm Market Road 1446 close to where we once lived. The hair on my arms and legs are gone. Eyebrows. What little hair was on my head is now a memory; what's left of my beard smells like a dead farm animal.

As I stood up, my clothes are burnt off as well. Naked as a jaybird. I start my walk home smelling like cow shit, covered from head to toe. Now to find something to cover myself with. Luckily I find a wet cardboard box to cover me. Somewhat. As I continue on, people on Interstate 35e are blowing their horns at me. I'm waving with my middle finger, saying howdy back. Now I reach home after a two-hour walk, half frozen to death. Feet are killing me. I happen to see the porch light is on. I screamed. Sherry had called and had the power fixed at an enormous rate, I find out later on. Went to open the door. It's locked. Another wait and finally Sherry opens the door, smiling at my dumb ass.

I didn't mutter a word. Straight to the shower to remove all this yuck from my body. For two more days I didn't utter a word. Now Christmas is over. Hallelujah. She starts taking her pretties down and boxing them up for Steve to put back in the attic—a happy chore for me. Got my TV back. I'm a happy man again. Till next year, my friends.

A Moment in Time

A new story (a moment in time). As the leaves begin to fall in October of 1880 in a small town in northern Texas, a young boy wakes as he hears the grandfather clock in the living room strike midnight beyond the small post office on a street covered with freshly built two-story homes his dad and some of his friends had built with money borrowed from Waxahachie Bank and Trust, which stood until the early 1900s. It was taken by fire sadly with many people's money as well. Their home still stands today in all its beauty, red in color with a wraparound porch all trimmed in white.

As sixteen-year-old Jesse walks down the glorious staircase that starts at the top at four feet wide and winds down almost in a complete circle reaching the living room, six feet wide. The rails to the staircase are made of handcrafted cherrywood. It's astounding the craftsmanship that was put into just one of the most detailed homes I'll ever see. You can hear every footstep as he tries to be so quiet.

He is the oldest of eight children. The floors are polished in a high sheen that his mother keeps up along with raising his four sisters and three younger brothers. His dad is a farmer raising cotton, wheat, corn, and soy bean, on Farm Road 1446 six miles west of town,. He peeks into his father and mother's bedroom to see them fast asleep. The door creaks ever so slightly as he closes it behind him. Jesse loves helping his dad plow the five hundred acres they own that has been passed down for generations. Jesse is so very proud to be the oldest.

At 3:00 a.m. he saddles his horse to get an early start to the land. The wind out of the north is very brisk for a October morning. He arrives at their land an hour later, pushing his horse Blue Boy all the way. A small barn stands for their two plow horses, which walk behind the plow with burlap bags of winter wheat seed, which needs to be in the ground soon. First, he unsaddles Blue Boy and gives some fresh hay to all three horses, leans back on a bale of hay and starts writing in his journal with only a lantern for light.

As 4:00 a.m. soon approaches, his dad and younger sister wake. Sara is fourteen years old. As she dresses for the chilly morning, she puts on a pair on long johns, a wool sweater, a pair of jeans, and two pairs of socks and pulls her boots on. Her coat reaches to her feet, black in color. She wears a felt cowboy hat beige in color pulled down as far as you can imagine. She then pulls her long brunette hair out from her hat that hangs down to the middle of her back. She stands five feet ten inches tall, a beauty inside and out with a hardworking ethic at one so young.

They begin to hitch the team of horses to a wagon. Dad knows not to look for Jesse in their home. He knows Jesse is already there. As Sara and their dad approach their land, they can see Jesse plowing. As the sun begins to crest over the flat farmland, you can see for miles.

Years would pass. Jesse refuses to sell the land while others gave up their heritage. Jesse is now sixty-three years old. His four sons work the land that will never be sold. Most farmers in Ellis County sold their land to developers to break up the land and build homes that now has made this country weak. Farmers across Texas are giving in and selling off what was once a tradition to make money at what their parents and grandparents worked so hard to keep in the family.

For the forty-plus years Sherry and myself have lived here raising our children. It saddens me to see every few months more farmland being sold for housing or new businesses that are a constant growth. I personally know two of Jesse's sons who still work the land through drought, many wet winters where their seeds rot in the ground, yet they won't give in. Waxahachie will never be what it once was—a small town where everyone knew each other. Now I rarely see anyone I once knew. I remember when it was a town of seven thousand people, now has grown into forty thousand, when your word was all you needed to make an agreement. A handshake meant more than any signed paper—this moment has now passed.

I dedicate this story to every farmer across this land who refuses to sell and keeps us from going hungry. Thank y'all for reading.

Steve Summers

A Waterbed and Two Monkeys

This is an old, true story I wrote a few years ago—LOL could it called a day of days

In 1983 we bought our first and only waterbed. It has survived three homes. This is the third mattress. When you move, a new mattress is a given—hopefully reaching its final destination.

For a few years my bride wanted to move it in our bedroom, turning it in another direction. Finally last Saturday I gave in. I've made many mistakes in my lifetime, and boy howdy was this one—so we start at 7:00 a.m.

First, draining trouble starts. We couldn't get all the water out. It's filled with foam as well. So we roll the mattress from the frame into the floor with many attempts. It's heavier than six dead bodies taped together. Gasping for air, we both are already worn out. Break time. Now noon arrives. I'm thinking, "What have I got myself into?"

Back to work, removing the headboard next, then the pads from the sides—now time to stand the bed frame up and figure out where to put it in our bedroom so it doesn't get in the way of the new location, scratching our heads like two monkeys with dumb looks on our faces. A place is found after much thought. Standing the bed frame up a chore in itself. Sliding it across the carpet and leaning in a corner. Now the support box, which holds the bed up. Measuring time to make sure it's in the center of the room. Absolutely the easiest part of this whole mess.

Sherry wants to vacuum where the bed once set. Outside I go to wonder if this day will ever end. Now 2:00 p.m., pissed and wanting to choke myself, so I decide to go feed our lab Coco and try to console myself as much as possible, sitting in my shop, not wanting to go back into our home. At 3:00 p.m. I make my way back in to see what's next. Sherry has moved all the dressers and her bookshelves into their new places. She has many books, all hardbacks she's bought through the years, a very avid reader. Everything is dusted as well.

Impressed I was and a little ashamed. I was outside and feeling guilty. So I get my second wind as she's about to fall out yet ready to start putting the bed in place, which we do also the headboard. Now time to get the mattress back in the bed. Mercy. Both of us are down on our knees pulling and tugging to get the mattress back in the bed frame. Break time once more. Not successful yet. Sherry goes back in. Before she leaves, she tells me of an idea. I say have at it. Two minutes later I go back in. There she sits in the bathroom sucking on the water hose to get more water out.

At this point anything is better than doing what we're doing. Didn't work. Back on our knees. With everything we have in us left, which isn't much. We are victorious the mattress is now in the bed frame. We both fall to the floor, panting for air, worn out. Another break. Now 5:00 p.m. the mattress is upside down. Many words came from my mouth I will not mention. Turning the mattress over is a feat beyond belief. Finally, success is made. Break time once more. Now 7:00 p.m., excited we were. Sticking the water hose back through the window to fill it up. As the bed fills, we eat to gain some strength back. At 8:00 p.m. the bed is full of water. At 9:00 p.m. we go to bed. It's colder than you could imagine. And no we didn't forget to plug the heater in for the bed.

Normally it takes two days for it to reach its correct temperature. So we just grin at each other and freeze until Sunday morning. End of story.

Where y'all goin'? It ain't over yet.

The next day at 9:00 p.m. after breakfast, the mattress is not in the frame as it should be. Sherry says, again draining—what a drag.

This time a different approach is taken by Steve. Getting almost all the water out. Then we pretty much are able to move the mattress where it was designed to go. Amen—now noontime for football. I fall asleep and miss more than I watched. Two monkeys together can do anything. Proven. My bride, Sherry Summers, was right. We now have twice the space we had before. As far as moving it again, it will never happen in my lifetime or hers. Ask her if you don't believe me! That's all, folks.

A Nightmare on Panorama Loop

Last week my bride, Sherry Summers, was working second shift due to a hearing test they have. Thursday at Purrzackly twelve high noon. She left for work. So I walked out to her car and kissed the sweet little woman she is goodbye. I went to go back to our home.

She had locked me out. Rage it was. I jumped in my truck and grabbed my trusty nine-millimeter Glock pistol and got off three rounds before she turned the corner, blowing out the back window. She turned in the middle of our street and headed back. I panicked and dove through a window in the computer room, sustained only small cuts. I then locked every door and hid in the attic, sweating like a pet coon in the Sahara Desert, had to be 140 degrees up there.

After an hour, I thought I heard her car start and leave—wrong. As I climbed down from the attic, taking each step with extreme caution and letting the door to the attic close very gently, there she stood with a baseball bat. First swing got me in the knees. As I went down, I remember one across my back, then knocked unconscious with a blow to my head. Woke up hours later chained to a shed I'd built years earlier for our dogs. Coco was licking me in the face with her teeth needing brushed. Mercy, bad breath.

Later that evening Sherry arrived home. She watered down Coco, fed her, leaving the dog food far from my reach. I was livid, hurting and sweating from a one-hundred-degree day. The next day once again she did the same for Coco, then threw a can of raw bisques. Uhhhhh from my reach. I scrambled to get a taste. Gone in a flash. I watched Coco devour the whole can, paper and all. I thought, "What kind of woman does this to her husband!" A scorned and pissed-off woman, I guess.

The third day starving, stinky, dehydrated I found an old file in the dirt and began filing away at a thick chain that I had placed there years ago. After many hours, I cut myself loose, my right hand bleeding so bad from using the file, kicked in the back door in and bandaged my hand. Off to the refrigerator I ran, drinking water like it's the first I'd ever had, water pouring from both sides of my mouth as I drank and drank, then eating everything in sight. Eventually a shower to clean off all signs of a dog that covered me. Got in my chair, turned the AC to super-cool, and fell asleep—if there is a next time, I'll make sure my empty head is fully packed with straw. Who am I kidding? Yep, there will be a next time of some kind or another.

Some hours later I heard the door to the garage close. I played possum as she entered the living room. She kissed me on the head and said, "How ya doin'?" Smiling she was. I never uttered a word. Sleeping once again with one eye open. Woke up to a fine meal she had prepared. I ask, "Can I eat?" "Sure," she said. Happy again to be in marital bliss.

There is a moral to this story. If you're going to shoot at your spouse, at least wound them and this won't happen to you. I like it inside—that's all I got to say about that.

Steve "Scarecrow" Summers

A Story

Imagine a world without hunger, no wars, living in peace for the rest of everyone's life. Possible. Yes, it is. Freedom to speak your mind in every country, freedom restored to what we once held so dear, never to be taken away ever again—to go to any country and feel safe, no terrorist, no robbery, murder, rape—a safe environment for all. Free medical treatment, no more monopoly on pharmaceutical companies, government officials, and politicians including the president. No more than a four-year term to be held in office. A 10 percent flat tax for everyone including billion-dollar companies throughout the world.

Money then would be abundant for all to pay their debts, no tax on gasoline, food, cars etc. Abolish the IRS, not needed in a perfect world—homes that were seized by mortgage companies to be given back to our soldiers, that we as Americans bailed out with no respect for what we've done for them. Close them down if not complied with the needs of hardworking people of all countries. No more inflation (freeze) and pay enough so what needs bought can be purchased. Children running and playing outside with no prejudice of any kind, never to notice skin color of anyone. Also treating their parents with the respect like we did as children. A different time and surely a different era. Grown-ups acting like they should. Instead of the children they once were years ago. Freedom to attend any church of your liking. Worship in your own way while keeping your heart close to your beliefs, not someone else's. And last yet not least, live in harmony as we should.

I will close now. John Lennon was a dreamer such as I. You may say these things are not possible, but they are only if we change.

A Trip to DC

When I was nine years old, I started having questions about what Dad did in WW II. Not much at all from him about it, of what he saw and had done. On a summer day Dad asked if we would all like to go to DC. I was eager to see somewhere new and learn about Washington.

Mom packed an old Coleman steel cooler with plum rose ham, bologna chips, etc. Off we went, stopping at a roadside park in Pennsylvania after driving for many hours it seemed. I loved the ham, chips, and Cokes in the six and a half bottles from those days Mom had brought along for our journey.

Entering DC we went under the Potomac River through a tunnel. This was so neat for a nine-year-old. Looking out the back window, I was taken that this was possible. It was dark as we entered Washington. The lights from the Capitol were glowing. I was impressed already. Mom had booked us a hotel downtown. I was up before anyone the next morning, ready to venture out and see everything.

First, we went for breakfast then made our way to the Capitol. First watching the changing of the guards at the unknown soldiers tomb. These men never moved an eye or blinked. Such training to achieve this, I thought. On to where John F. Kennedy was buried and see the eternal flame burning bright. Dad mentioned he'd like to go to Arlington National Cemetery next. I stayed by his side through this to see his reaction. It was one of a man with a somber look on his face. I heard him wince as he kneeled at a grave.

That's when I stood back and gave Dad his privacy. Many times as we walked through the cemetery, I saw tears in Dad's eyes. It made me cry as well. I hid them from everyone. This was his day, not mine. After leaving there, a tour through the White House, everything so clean and polished you could see yourself in the tile that lay on the floor. Portraits hung of past presidents on the walls. One in particular caught my eye. JFK's portrait. I can still see in my mind. Folded arms. Looking like a man with too much on his mind. I believe he had good things planned for this country before his death. Paul Harvey was a visionary, seeing the world as it is now from his perspective in the sixties. I feel the same way about JFK.

After returning home, Dad talked a little of the war, teaching me a little German he had picked up while serving this country. Never did he say anything about the battles he was in and the death he saw or if he had killed anyone.

Alzheimer's

Bill Jennings was born to Maggie and Paul Jennings on November 21, 1926, in Tyler, Texas. Bill's dad was a crop duster all around the Tyler area. Back then farmland was about all you could see in any direction. As Bill grew, his dad would take him with him in the plane, an old two-seater biplane. By the time Bill was seven, he was flying with his dad at the controls for the most part with his dad watching his every move. Imagine now, if you can, how time slips away from us all.

Bill is now seventeen years old and a very good pilot. He joins the navy and with more training becomes a fighter pilot, a good-looking young man, six feet tall, sandy blond hair, and wants to kill Germans so our soldiers on the ground will be much safer, which he does. On a dangerous mission, Bill is shot down in a field in Normandy. Four Germans find him and are carrying him back to German intelligence when they come across a patrol of American paratroopers who kill them and carry Bill to a ship where he is badly wounded. In less than three months he's back flying again.

The war ends, and Bill lands a job as a pilot for Delta airlines. This is where he meets Annie, a stewardess, and falls in love. They marry and have three children, a boy, Bill Junior, and two girls, Mary and Patricia. As time passes, Annie is killed in a car wreck in 1979. Bill is beside himself with grief and never fully recovers from losing her. Bill paces the floor for months to come. He is completely lost without Annie.

Bill finally starts going to a local restaurant in Tyler, reminiscing with a friend from the war. One morning he gets ready to go meet his friends and can't remember how to get there. He drives in circles.

He is stopped at the light and can't remember to go on green or red. The police pull up and ask him, "What is wrong with you?" Bill has no answer, sits there talking to himself. The police handcuff Bill and take him to jail. His car is towed also. Finally after a night in jail his children come and get their dad Bill Jr., takes his car home, and park it and keep the keys. Bill is now eighty-nine years old, does not know his children or anyone. He stays with his son the remainder of his life. At ninety-one years old he passes away in the night to go home to Annie.

Casualties

In the spring of 1998 twin girls were born to Karen and Jeff McDowell in Durant, Oklahoma. At forty years old Karen was sure she'd never have any children. She had been told from the beginning of her marriage to Jeff she couldn't get pregnant. She was so happy to have twin girls. They were loved beyond belief from both parents.

Karen and Jeff agreed on their names, Keri and Sherri. They were adorable. As kids growing up they were inseparable. Both were good students, loved by everyone they met. On graduation in May of 2016, they walked together side by side, holding hands, down the long aisle on the way to receive their diplomas. A year passed. Keri was married to her high school sweetheart Mike Bourne, also a native of Durant. He took over his dad's business at a well-respected chain of grocery stores throughout Oklahoma. After a short battle with a brain tumor Mike's dad was gone. The small town was in mourning of such a tragic loss.

Sherri went from one small-paying job to another not knowing what her future had in store for her. She read an article where in Seattle, Washington, the minimum wage had been raised to fifteen dollars an hour. Sherri was impressed. She wanted out of Durant for good. At 1:00 a.m. while her mom and dad were fast asleep, she packed her clothes, a few snacks from the refrigerator, and headed to the bus stop. As she waited, a calm covered her. She was excited to be leaving. At 2:00 a.m. the bus arrived on schedule to carry her far away. As morning broke, her mom and dad awoke and called out, "Sherri, come to breakfast, you're going to be late for work." No answer.

Karen went running to her room. In an instant Karen was frantic, searching their home for Sherri. Jeff was on the phone with the local police. They told him she is not a minor. "We can't do nothing for twenty-four hours." Jeff threw the phone through the living room window crying. As Karen entered the living room, she was crying also. Both made posters and copies reaching two hundred, posting them all over town, with no response from anyone. The media arrived from Oklahoma City the next day interviewing Karen and Jeff, pleading for her to come home.

Two weeks passed. An all-out search was conducted in the woods with over three hundred people. Friends, family, caring citizens never found a clue. After a month, everyone gave up except Karen, Jeff, and her sister Keri. Keri's marriage became rocky after many sleepless nights. At this point she didn't care what happened as long as Sherri was found safe.

Sherri arrived in Seattle with a few hundred dollars she had saved to have a fresh start, found a flea bag motel at a reasonable rate per day, went on a search for a job. First interview lands a job at a local steakhouse with great tips. Starting pay fifteen dollars an hour. Within a month Sherri has her own apartment. Winter is on its way, turns bitter cold. Sherri learns quickly she doesn't like all the freezing rain. She becomes depressed. One night after work she is walking home to her apartment. Freezing a good mile away she collapses on Seventh Street and Main. A local Good Samaritan stops his car, backs up, puts Sherri in the back seat, and speeds to a local hospital. She is somewhat coherent as she is taken to ICU for treatment. In her purse her ID is found, driver's license number 75160478, an Oklahoma license.

Her skin is ripped away from most of her face and any open area on her body. The Seattle police arrive at the hospital to run a check in Oklahoma for a Sherri McDowell. The Oklahoma police tell them she has been missing for months. Her parents are called. Karen and Jeff fly to Seattle to see their daughter who was presumed dead. Sherri is unrecognizable to her parents, yet they know this is her. After three months of intense surgeries from a good plastic surgeon, she is looking like herself again. Mom and dad never leave her side. Sister Keri flies up with husband Mike. Mike is now understanding the bond these two twin sisters share, never to be broke.

Sherri is put in rehab learning to walk again, her sister, Keri, helping her each day and night. Six months has passed. Sherri is walking just a she once did. Her voice is some different from the bitter cold on that lonely walk home. She decides to move back to Oklahoma and go to college and get her degree in ER care for victims of almost her own demise. The steakhouse owner pays all bills from the hospital reaching seven hundred thousand dollars. After two years of college, Sherri returns to Seattle to provide care for anyone she possibly can. She is an example to others to this very day. She walks nowhere now. She drives a brand-new Porsche Carrera bought with her own money. The end.

From the empty head of a scarecrow with little straw to work with. I'm a thinkin' I need a new bale of straw right real soon! Anything is possible when you open your heart up to friends. Dedicated to a good friend my sunflower good friend. A lovely day to you. Steve Summers. That's all, folks.

Cut from a Familiar Cloth

As the days turn into years, my life is passing quicker than imaginable—for some of us, maybe more. Childhood days were better than good as I reflect on mine. Mom stayed home, cooked, and cleaned, made sure we had enough to eat. We went to church on Sunday, taken to the doctor for regular checkups—the list goes on and on about what they sacrificed for us kids when they did without. My dad worked hard every day outside the mines, driving a Euclid truck on dirt roads not fit for nothing to be driven on through the rain and snow, yet he did this for four kids so we could have enough. We were never rich by any means, but the love they showed to each of us was plenty enough for me. They both had an impact on my life I still carry today.

This story I dedicate to the ones who weren't shown what we were as a family.

Distance

Over the years I've distanced myself from many lost friends and things that have happened to me along in my life. Yet James "Pug" Elswick and Wayne Newsome I can't seem to ever get them off of my mind. More than once a week they both are in my thoughts, and I wonder what they would be like today. I see Wayne living in Kentucky close to his dad with his wife and four children, grandchildren running and playing. He would have loved to see this. I know in my heart.

Wayne was a good person with morals and a high standard in family values. Wayne's dad was a huge influence in both our lives, loving cars as he taught us how to work on Pontiacs, like Firebirds and GTOs. Speed was the key for Wayne and me. I loved his dad like my own, and he loved me like a son. Erwin is still alive and living in Inez, Kentucky. What I wouldn't give to pull in his driveway and stay for days and talk of Wayne, cars, and what we've both been doing for forty-one years. I miss so much of all the Newsome family I cannot put into words.

A little secret that's never been told. On a sunny day we were riding around in my '69 GTO. We headed toward Kopperston Mountain, laughing as we hit the mountain doing ninety miles an hour, listening to Charlie Daniels in an old eight-track player. I looked over at him and said, "Let's go to Wharton and blow this car out." On a long, straight away I nailed it to the floor, with one slick tire on the front, and the others weren't much better. The GTO was registered for 160 miles per hour. On this day we hit 150 miles per hour, before the valves in the engine began to float. So I shut it down and coasted it to about one hundred. We had no fear of anything. Always thinking we were invincible.

I know this is why we were the way we were. Little did we know shortly after this crazy stunt Wayne would be—I can't say the word as the tears leak down my face. As I learned of Wayne's fate, I remember going home to Mom and Dad's and laying my head in my daddy's lap and crying like a schoolchild who had lost everything. For me that night I had. I now try and think of only the good times and not the end of his life. It consumed me for many months. Nothing seemed to help me through these times, eventually moving on without him. We shared so much together I cannot write it all. We were both born in Kentucky and shared the same birthday. Only one year apart. I am the oldest.

On this remembrance of his life I left out our childhood on purpose. I have written of it before. It also was a memory of joy. If you would like to read of this, you are welcome to go back to a story from a year ago—I'll keep to myself on this day. This story will go public for more of Wayne's friends to see who remembers him, who I'm not friends with. I have also picked out a song for Wayne as I've done for James for many years, which will be posted later and dedicated to him, for I do not know if that will be possible or if I'll come back to Facebook for a day or two.

My knees are buckling. I seek no pity in this story. I can't help the way I feel or my heart works. So I will end it here. To know Wayne Newsome was to only love him.

Fire Starter

In the summer of 1975, twin boys were born to Stacie and John Hugh in Rockwood, Tennessee, on June 27. They were premature, only given a fifty-fifty chance of survival. After three long months, they were finally released to go home. Both parents had prayed over them countless times. Stacie had cried her eyes out waiting and waiting. She never left their side. John was a painter and would go straight to the hospital every day after work, a long ten-hour day. Their names are Jim and James. At three years old the boys were fighting as siblings sometimes do. They were a mess at age seven, getting into trouble in the first grade.

Stacie and John busted their butts on a regular basis, trying so hard to teach them right from wrong at a very early age with not much success. At age ten, James started straightening up. Jim, on the other hand, had no intention of doing nothing but what he wanted. In appearance they were identical. At fifteen years old both boys had a bond that was inseparable. Both had now learned what their parents said was gospel: you either toe the line or Dad would loosen his belt, and they knew what was coming.

On a cold afternoon in 1990 they wandered into the woods too far from home to find their way back for five days.

Fire

In 1995 on a cold January night at 2:00 a.m. our home phone rang. When I answered, someone said get to the Waxahachie ER now, no time for asking questions. I put on some clothes and was there in minutes. I went to the front desk and asked who they had. They said your brother. I screamed "Open the doors."

I found Carl sitting in a room shivering with second-degree burns on his head and back, plus third-degree burns on his arm. I spotted a doctor and was screaming at him to get his ass in there and treat Carl. He just stood there. Then I got up and got in his face to see about my brother. Nothing. Security came and threatened to throw me out. Did not happen. Finally the doctor came to the exam room and said, "What's the problem?"

Carl and I were livid. Carl looked so pitiful, his shirt burnt off his back. Shaking, hurting, I started crying and told the dumbass doctor, "He needs morphine now." Still nothing. The doctor left the exam room. A nurse came in, and I pleaded with him to give him some morphine. The nurse said he was mad as hell at the doctor and couldn't do it without the doctor's orders. All the nurses were mad. Finally, after an hour passed, he was given morphine and transferred to Parkland hospital in Dallas, one of the best burn units in America.

Carl's nurse told us before we left for Parkland the so-called doctor almost let a five-year-old child die a week earlier. We arrived at Parkland at around 5:00 a.m. They hurried him back to surgery. Two burn doctors worked on Carl for three hours, taking skin from his leg to put on his arm, giving him more morphine for the pain. At 8:30 a.m. he went to recovery and slept. I was told what had to be done then. Sherry came and picked me up at around nine that morning. We went to Waxahachie to get my truck. I napped for a while and back to Dallas I flew to check on him.

Carl was conscious in a private room smiling at me and said, "I thought you were going to jail." "No, you're my only concern." For many days and evenings I sat with him, carrying him *Hot Rod* magazines—anything he wanted. All our aunts showed up to see him—Velma, Mary, Sylvia, Violet that live in Texas, and friends as well. After a week they released Carl to mine and Sherry's care. I changed his bandages after he would take a lukewarm bath every morning. It seemed as painful for me as it did him. After three weeks Carl went and stayed with a neighbor. He was on the mend somewhat. While he was staying with us, he asked if Sherry and I would go to his home and salvage what we could, something I was dreading.

As we pulled up to his home, it was gutted. I started with tears rolling down my face, looking for anything of value that was left. All his albums that were autographed were burnt up but one. Clothes were smoke damaged. All his furniture was gone, washer and dryer. I looked and looked for some good news, never to be found. My heart was in tears as my eyes were. Money was given from his friends from work. I went to convince stores, grocery stores, with glass jars to collect money for Carl. Very little was given at any store. The steel front door that had burnt his hands was melted in the corners. Pretty much everything was burnt up. He lived in a rent home with no renter's insurance.

Sherry and I bought him some shirts and jeans, underwear, plus a coat. He stayed with Mac, his neighbor, for quite a while, a good man who was widowed and liked Carl so much, later moved to Alvarado, Texas, after that and rented a double-wide where he still lives today. It is about a thirty-minute drive from Waxahachie. Twenty-two years later he wears a special sock to cover his arm. No sunlight will ever shine on his arm again. Days passed then months and now years, forever embedded in my mind. I love him and would do anything to help him. He's my brother. Thank you to who may read this. Steve "Scarecrow" Summers. Please don't ask me any questions out of respect!

Funding

I'm guessing it was last weekend or sometime in the last month. Not real sure, memory is a far gone conclusion anymore. I'm still and will always keep stuffing straw in my head to stay a little more alert, yet there are times it just doesn't work as well as I wished. I bought a Powerball ticket worth 320 million dollars. Anyhoot I checked it this past Saturday night. Seems a guy from Waxahachie, Texas, won and yours truly. It was me. With much excitement headed home to tell my bride. Troubles be gone.

I was told by my daughter fifteen years ago I would win big someday after winning thirty thousand on a two-dollar scratch-off ticket in April of the year 2000. A long wait it was. Not no more. Our minds were rushing with ideas. Then finally I said. A Lear jet is what we need and we'll fly ourselves to West Virginia to see Mom. Looking on the internet for Lear jets, we found them at Meacham air base in Fort Worth. They had plenty to choose from. So off we go after a quick stop at Dallas and bought a Lamborghini to drive to Fort Worth, seven hundred horsepower with a six-speed manual transmission. Styling now. We're pulling up pavement as we drive to Fort Worth, arriving in record time.

We start our search. Having around forty to choose from. My eyes glazed at a triple black in color. Exterior with cream leather interior, two beds, fully stocked bar, two TVs, computers, shower stall. Top speed nine hundred miles an hour. Too much to list. Bought it. A problem with the FAA on granting me a pilot's license. That was an easier fix than I once thought at the time. Slipping them some funding eased their minds.

My bride was somewhat leery of our first flight. Me, nothing scares me. It was a breeze with autopilot and built-in landing. Though I did take the controls and did a few loops. Boy howdy. As good as when I jumped from a perfectly good plane years ago. A rush from eleven thousand feet I'll never forget. This may be better. Yep, it is. Then off to east Texas looking at land for a new home site, found five hundred acres with rolling hills, three ponds. Sizing from one acre to ten acres, pecan trees. Bought it. Our home will be designed by my bride. The only thing I'll have to do with the design of the home is a sixty-feet-by-sixty-feet game room with a nine-feet-by-five-feet pool table with pinball machines restored from the seventies, a Bose sound system to blast away my music. This room will be soundproof not to wake Sherry.

I'm looking at horses to ride and graze on this perfect piece of land. My new shop will be one hundred feet by two hundred feet with many classic cars and one '70 Chevy short wide bed pickup, all original, to be converted by me later with a 454,450 HP engine, tricked out to my satisfaction. An in-ground pool with built-in hot tub, slide, and diving board. We will visit our friends and enrich their lives as well.

Imagination is a terrible thing to waste. Use yours frequently. Thank you for your time.

Steve "Scarecrow" Summers

Graduation of 1975

It's been forty years since I walked the halls of Oceana High School. The time has gone by like a song I remember, time is here and gone. I remember so much of my friends and what we did as we went to school every day, except for the days we skipped and they were more than a few.

As a freshman I played the field then started dating a girl for a while, who ended up breaking my heart to date a senior, then on the loose to date, which I soon started, being attracted to many girls, yet I was a little shy. Then Laura comes to mind. Never did ask her out, should have, but I didn't. Once I met Jackie from Baileysville. We went out for a few times. Along comes Trish, another girl from Baileysville high school, had her own car, a Camaro. We dated for the rest of my freshman year.

Back then I had long, flowing black hair to my shoulders, which Mom complained of, yet I would never cut it and didn't. Sophomore year playing the field once again and running around with a friend, and we both were dating too many girls to name, and yes, we were wild as bucks and did things I'll leave out to protect us both. I sure do miss seeing my friend. It's been close to ten years now since we laid eyes on one another. I hope to fix this ASAP when Sherry and I make a trip to West Virginia in the near future. His mom thought I was a bad influence on him, and my mom thought the same of him. Neither of us cared what anyone thought. We did as we pleased and got away with most of it. So we thought. LOL.

I got my driver's permit that year at sixteen then my license. Poor ole Dad hitched a ride to work more than he drove because I wrecked just about everything he owned. Drinking and driving was not a good thing for my dad, for he was the one who suffered the most. A lesson learned. Both our children were bought their own cars. Times in the seventies most moms stayed home and dads worked. Our mom did not work. She was too busy looking after us four kids.

I ran track and loved it. As a junior we made the state finals and got to go to Beckley for a meet. Running on an asphalt track was something I'd never done before. Our track was dirt at OHS. Seems like I was faster with the soft asphalt under my feet. We placed fourth and fifth at the state meet. I was on three different relay teams. I still, to this day, have all my ribbons we won as a team. At the time being from a 1A school that was pretty good for us. After returning to school on a Monday, a sophomore I didn't like made a crack to me as I headed to another class as we met in the hall about our placing at the meet. All I remember is I punched him in the nose and pushed a sophomore into the boys' bathroom and started wailing on him. James "Pug" Elswick pulled me off of him. He was bloody from head down to his shirt collar,

I felt great I had stood up for our team. Now the bad news for Steve. I was carried to the principal's office and was given a choice of three days off or three licks from a very long and thick wooden paddle. Of course I opted out for the three days. Tuesday morning, Mom came in my bedroom to get me up for school. I told her there was something going on with the faculty and we were off until Friday. Didn't work out. Mom called the school and back I went to get my three licks. Dad gave me a little grin on the ride to Oceana while Mom was as red as hornet. My doom approached.

"Empty your back pockets," the principal said, "and I tell you this will hurt."

My junior year I lettered in track and received my letterman's coat, a very proud day. I wore it with pride and a feeling of accomplishment. A scholarship was awarded to me to attend Marshall university, which I declined. Thought welding was my ticket. Wrong again. Now every time I get an x-ray that is what I could have become, working in hospitals wherever I choose.

I had the best of both worlds in high school, hanging with the jocks as well as the potheads. Truthfully I smoked my share of weed running with some friends, also being a big flirt, LOL. Just me being me. Once I was dating a girl and then laid eyes on Sherry, sneaking around and pulling this off for a while, until getting caught. Then I had no girlfriend. After some pleading, I had Sherry back. She ended up being the love of my life and will forever be. We are complete opposites. Yet it works like no other marriage could. She is my soulmate. We walked to Rick's drive-in for lunch and hung with our best friends.

So much to reflect on. To go back now would be a dream come true and walk the halls of OHS. Seeing friends when we were all so young and carefree. We thought we were invincible the last day at Oceana High School, now seniors dressed in our caps and gowns, the final walk, a sobering thought for a few minutes as I marched with my classmates. Then I thought what a joy to be rid of this place.

Now in later years we are maybe not so glad to be rid of this place I find more and more each day as I lose friends from the class of 1975. Forty years will forever seem unreal, not seeing anyone from our class. We all went our separate ways as I chose to leave Oceana like others did as well.

Though we may be apart, many of you hold a special place in my heart. I pulled out my yearbook today and connected faces with names I'd long forgotten about. It was an eerie and sad feeling to know I'd never see them again. I will now read from our yearbook a few things. Our theme: "We shall never pass this way again." Our motto: "Give each day of life your best." Our colors: the rainbow. Flower: carnation.

In closing, I dedicate this story to all we have lost through the years. They are remembered. We never know when our day will come to join our friends that has departed this world. Then we will be only a memory. Sincerely, Steve Summers.

Hargie

As a seven-year-old growing up in Lynch, Kentucky, I had a friend. His name was Hargus "Hargie" Falls. He was a victim of down syndrome. I called him Hargie. His older brother by one year, Jimmy, would make fun of him—call him names, push him down. Even though Jimmy was bigger than me, I would beat Jimmy up. His mom, Geneva, would come out and pull us apart. She was as beautiful as they came. She and my mom were best friends. After we moved to West Virginia, I lost touch with every one of my friends.

I will always have a special place in my heart for anyone who has down syndrome. Every time I see a person with this dreaded disease, I always hug them and tell them how special they are to me, and I usually cry while when I tell them.

Steve

Hobo

As the sun rose to awaken me through the blinds, and as I stepped outside with coffee in hand, our home was reading ninety-eight degrees from the day before from the brick. It was one of those summers where temperatures were hitting in the 109 range, yet not as hot as the summer of 1997 when temperatures hit 116 degrees with a drought that lasted to October.

My day started by going to CVS in Red Oak to pick up some of my meds. As I neared the pharmacy, the sky opened with a shower of hard rain. Steam was rising from the concrete pavement six to eight inches high. As I entered the pharmacy, a man was sitting on the curb, drowning in sweat from the humidity and rain. I offered him five dollars, and he smiled as he took it. On the way home, I saw him walking toward Waxahachie, so I stopped and offered him a ride. Happy he was.

We talked some on my way home. He was headed to Waco, about seventy miles from our home. As we got close, I asked him if he would like to come home with me and shower and clean up some before his journey home. He said, "Yes, thank you." His face was worn with wrinkles from the sun and cold from many years on the road. His beard was long, part gray and red. He had but one set of other clothes. They were dirty as well. His boots were worn down to where his toes stuck out.

I was thinking what else I could do for him as he showered. Ideas started running through my mind. I had bought a pair of Nike Air tennis shoes I'd never worn. They hurt my feet even then. Also gave him three T-shirts, one pair of jeans, and two pairs of shorts.

He wept as we gathered his clothes up. I then brought him to Waco to see his brother.

Jim had been to just about every city you could name, not a lazy man. This was his life. As we arrived in Waco, he went inside and brought his brother out to meet me, very different from Jim, a man with a family, a wife, kids, and grandkids. As I left the driveway, tears ran down my face, not for what I had done, for helping someone in need.

Thank you for all that read this. Scarecrow Summers. Now make your choice. True or false.

Hourglass

The hourglass has now been turned over. As the sand begins to fall, two lifelong friends begin their quest to find their friend who has lost his way in the mountains of West Virginia close to Raleigh County in the winter of 1977.

Fresh snow has started to fall. It is bitter cold, and the snow is wet and slippery. As they search, they are calling out his name, Jim, over and over with no response. Minutes are slipping away. Darkness will be upon them soon. As they reach a ridge in the snow-covered mountains, Junior and Tom have to sit for a very few minutes to rest their tired bodies. Knowing they have little time, they rise and walk the ridge constantly yelling his name. They stop every minute or two and listen to hopefully hear Jim call back. With twenty-nine minutes of daylight left, they spot a small opening in the brush and trees that has blocked their way of seeing much of anything.

There lay Jim, unconscious from a fall he suffered from a rock formation. He is badly injured with a broken leg, head trauma. His fingers are starting to turn blue. They remove his gloves to check for a pulse. Jim is clinging to life. With no time to waste, Junior and Tom start their descent down the treacherous mountain they had climbed to find him. What you don't know is that Junior and Tom are worn out, yet they find broken branches and cut tree limbs to make a sled so they both can drag him out without hurting more than he already is. They cover him with their coats, trying to keep Jim warm.

Thirteen minutes to go before they will be in total darkness. They start running as fast as they can to get to safety before all three of them freeze to death. Junior slips and falls, breaking his wrist, telling no one. He bites his words in pain, still running to save their friend's life. Six minutes now remain. They are close yet need more daylight to find their way down, none of the three have flashlights.

Two minutes to go as the sun starts to settle beyond the vast mountains. They capture dim headlights at the bottom waiting for them to return. It's Jim's wife Carol waiting, crying as she sees them approaching. The hourglass has now emptied. All three were taken to a nearby hospital for exposure. Jim was treated. His release was two weeks later. Junior and Tom suffered frostbite. Junior never told anyone about his broken wrist, and to this day of January 24, 2019, has dealt with pain. They are still and will always be the best of friends.

For those of you that know me well and have read a few of my ironworking stories, there is nothing you wouldn't do to save a friend's life, even if it meant losing your own.

Humbled

Before I begin, I want whoever reads this to know it is all facts that I remember vividly. Starting in January 5, 2011, I was working at a plant that made foam for airplanes and boats. I'd been working there since August of 1999 as a welder/mechanic. In 2007 I was approached to take over chemical water testing. Got my degree in chemical engineering and started doing all the testing on boilers, cooling towers, adding chemicals and keeping them clean. I liked this job. There was a lot to learn, yet I caught on quickly.

On January 5, 2011, a pump blew in the boiler room. Two pumps were in place for backup in case one blew. So I and two of my coworkers went inside to change over to the other pump. As I changed valves to let the water flow into the secondary pump, it blew up, spraying hot water and steam in my face and right leg. I landed six feet away screaming like a child. I was rushed to Parkland hospital, a treatment of first and second burns to my right leg. I was burned from my waist to my knee. The most pain I'd ever felt in my life after the morphine kicked in—it was bearable.

After being released for Parkland, my sweet bride, Sherry Summers, would help me bathe. Removing the bandages was the hardest for me every morning. For three months I was on workers comp trying to heal. The fight began soon after being released to go back to work, and I did my rehab at home where I need to pay for my own medicine. Without me lying down on the floor and doing the exercise myself, I would today have a limb. On September 22, 2011, I was let go for fighting for insurance. A mere seven thousand dollars was awarded to me.

After going back and forth to the hospital for treatments to pull the dead skin from my leg. Pain no drugs at all, just lay there in the clean room as it was called and bore it. One day I showed up for treatment. In the lobby was a man with stints under each arm. His chest and arms had third-degree burns. Then I was humbled to have what my problems were. I bounced around for a while from job to job. Finally landing a job at an envelope factory in June of 2013. Didn't like it much, yet I stayed until January 16, 2014. They bitched about me checking my blood, which only takes a few seconds, going to the bathroom. I was already making half of the kind of money I was used to making in 2011. So I asked where do I sign to resign. Out the door I went. Called a lawyer and filed for disability.

After, over two years of waiting, doing some mowing for neighbors anything I could do to make a few dollars so I wouldn't have to ask Sherry for money. My truck was always on a quarter tank or less. We were in jeopardy of losing our home. We ate whatever and was happy to have it. Glad to have anything to eat. I lost my manhood, thought of suicide. I was a mess.

Sherry kept on plugging at her job. Knowing this made it hard for me to walk her to the garage. As she drove away, I felt like I had failed as a husband. She knew different. In my mind I wasn't convinced. We hung together and made it through some of the worst times of our marriage—strong marriages survive, and ours is stronger than anything on earth. Now with my back pay and monthly check, we have started home improvements. Buying new clothes for ourselves. New pillows was one of my favorites. Towels. Sheets for our water bed. I never realized how worn out mine was until I sunk my head into a new one.

I'm humbled to know now knowing what you can survive together. I know in my heart there are people out there much worse off than we were. Feels good to be living again.

Illusions

Lucy Gentry was born in 1836 in the flat hills of California to Elizekel and Caroline Gentry with three brothers she adored. Her dad supported his family from panning for gold in the small streams that surrounded their small log cabin.

By 1850 Lucy left home and went out on her own to seek her fortune. She was just fourteen years of age and had a knack for finding gold. On her sixteenth birthday on October 10, 1852, she began to see things while sleeping on a rolled-out blanket in the woods of California. She would wake from these dreams trembling not knowing what was happening to herself.

Lucy was not educated much at all, only what her mother had taught her about adding and subtracting. She knew nothing of the world before her time. On a dark night with only firelight to see with, she heard rustling in the trees and branches near her fire. As she looked closer, she saw a Roman soldier ride by her fire. The horse snorted as they passed. She was terrified not knowing what this was or who. Lucy heard the brass clicking from the soldier's uniform, ran and hid behind a tree.

Two years would pass, and the dreams continued. She didn't understand any of this, only wanted to be free of it all, not to be. On her twentieth birthday she had a vision of Egyptians building the pyramids in the days before Christ was born. She could see every stone being placed in perfect alignment as the slaves pulled while being whipped. Lucy knew none of this, never taught. At age thirty the gold had panned out for just about everyone except Lucy who was guided by a force she knew nothing of, yet reaped the benefits, became a rich woman.

She settled in San Francisco, bought a hotel, and lived like a queen until her untimely death at age fifty-seven on her birthday, October 10, 1893—a visionary maybe. What Lucy saw—illusions, I don't think so. She was gifted from God and was saved by his grace. Thank you for reading.

Scarecrow

Impact

For many years I've been a dreamer and a wanderer, dreaming of a better world, wondering why things are the way they are in all countries. When 9-11 happened, I wondered why these planes were not shot out of the air. Everyone knows or should know they were in no-fly zones, yet they weren't shot down, and thousands died. Because of this, now years later, friends and families still mourn the loss of their loved ones, who were killed. Not only in the US. Many countries lost as well, those in the Twin Towers. Its impact on those are unimaginable, and maybe some of you, yes firefighters, police, pedestrians who tried to help, as the buildings collapsed on them as well.

Now close your eyes for one moment and see if you can see one person who lost their life on this day and try and imagine the impact it still and will forever have on a wife, a husband, a child, a cousin, a father, a mother. It goes on and on. Never ending. Without words I'm at a loss wondering. Why!

In Her Arms

Ann Blevins and Mike Cooper were born on the same day in April 25, 1970, in Wichita, Kansas. As years passed, they attended preschool together, then grade school. Once in high school, they began a romance that grew. They both attended Kansas State University.

Ann received her doctorate in mathematics and became a college professor at Kansas State. Mike would get his degree in architectural design. They married on March 1, 1995, in their hometown. After twelve years of marriage with no children, their jobs became more important than being husband and wife. Separated for one year and filed for divorce. Something they thought would never happen to them. So love had now faded away.

Mike moved on and remarried. Ann couldn't find her way, depressed, falling apart mentally, physically, dropped to ninety pounds. At five feet eight inches tall she looked bad. Her friends didn't know how to comfort her. She was a mess and getting worse. Ann's best friend, Melissa, talked her into seeing a doctor for her depression. Little by little she came back to her old self, put her twenty pounds back on, was looking like she did before. She was now on the road to recovery and having fun with going out, wearing makeup, which she didn't really need. Ann was a runner-up in Miss America as a seventeen-year-old, beautiful then and now.

Ann never got over Mike. On a date at a café, she spotted Mike and his wife. As a few tears ran down her face, she tried to control them so her date couldn't see them. Six weeks passed. Ann and Mike ran into each other at a local merchandize mart and began a conversation on how they were doing. Mike realized he was still in love with Ann. A month passed. Mike told his wife Sara it was over between them, divorced her, packed his bags, gave Sara their home, and left to get Ann back in his arms once again.

Ann was elated to know she would be back with Mike. It happened, married on the same day and month they were before. The romance grew to heights you can only imagine. They were taking trips together, a new life for them both. It was like heaven on earth for them, worked out something that was once standing in the way, no more. They will be together forever in their eyes and are today on December 6, 2018.

Thank y'all for reading.

Scarecrow

Inside the Line

On one of my many trips to West Virginia to visit my lovely mom, I decided to go in October to see the leaves change and spend my forty-seventh birthday with her. My sister Sarah was driving. My head was spinning like a top looking at everything as we passed by on the way there. We rode to Twin Falls State Park. The leaves were just as I had remembered from years ago. Perfect. We saw deer on the road, an adventure I'll forever hold close to my heart. If I could only describe to you what it meant to me.

The week flew by in a flash. Leaving Mom is the hardest thing I will ever do. I was crying as we drove away. I never looked back, put my sunglasses on, and walked away with tears flowing from under my sunglasses. Sam and Sarah brought me back to Charleston to fly back to Dallas. We stopped at a restaurant for something to eat. As I sat down, I had a feeling I'd never felt before. I went to the restroom and tried to throw up. I ended up outside standing trying to figure out what was wrong with me as they ate.

Arriving at the airport we said our goodbyes. I bought a Sprite to try and settle my stomach. Didn't work. Boarding a Lear jet to Charlotte, I sat down in my seat a few rows back. As the plane taxied down to take off, I asked if the person in the solo seat would trade with me. I wanted to be alone if possible. He said yes. As we passed in the aisle, it was a friend from Gilligan's Island. I only thanked him. Later I learned he had cancer and was going to Charlotte for treatment. Never before in my life after arriving in Charlotte, the ride from there to Dallas was the longest flight ever, two and a half hours, which seemed like nothing before.

Sherry picked me up. I told her I wasn't feeling well at all. The next day, which was a Sunday, I didn't want to be around Jake or Sherry. All I wanted was fixed. I went to work Monday, could not look anyone in the eye, just paced and tried to stay out of sight. Many friends tried talking with me. I just couldn't. Also, if there was more than one person in line at a convenience store I walked out. Finally, after no sleep for days, I went and saw my doctor. He sat me up with a radiologist, did every kind of test known to man.

So I went back to my doctor. He sat me down and asked what was going on in my life, so I told him. Then he knew. Prescribed Clonazepam, a low dose, for anxiety. It worked and is still working thirteen years later. I will admit I was loopy for a while. Then I figured out I didn't need three pills a day. Sherry bought a pill cutter, and I would only take what I needed to calm me down, again a little peace in my life. Three years later at fifty years old, I go in for a cololoscopy.

The blood work shows I have diabetes. I'm astounded and pissed. I thought by sixty-eight I'd have dirt covering me. The point to all this is when my anxiety goes up my blood sugar goes up with it—options: insulin and half a pill. So if you see me close my Facebook down, now you know why. Sometimes I get so caught up in the music my blood follows and I'm logging off—the good news we go out to eat, concerts whatever we want to do.

Don't give up. I know I almost did and ended it all. Thank you for your time.

Steve "Scarecrow" Summers

Ironworking

In the spring of 1983, forty ironworkers were called into the union hall, including myself, to discuss two projects going up simultaneously, one off of Wycliff Street and the other on Lemon and Oaklawn Avenue. The one off Wycliff was a hotel seventeen stories tall and was a Lowes Anotle hotel and had to be finished by late October of 1984 for the Republican national convention. Ronald Reagan was running for president. The push was on. It was a cost plus job where we were paid above our regular salary.

After a brutal winter hit, ice storms were everywhere that year. As we reached the thirteenth floor, lightning was striking the iron. A fellow ironworker was struck, killing him instantly. Two of us made our way to him. His body was black. The tips of his boots were blown off. I screamed on the radio to send a basket from the 4100 Manitowoc crane below, a pause while I gathered myself. The next day Curt and I were sent to the Claradiage off Oaklawn and Lemon hopefully to clear our head a little, a condominium that was ten stories high with eight stories underground for parking for the tenants who would buy one once it was finished. Starting price $450,000, which was only for the rich in 1983.

On this job there was no room for error. Heavy traffic surrounds us. A few days passed. The ice was gone. Then came the heavy rain. I was considered a connector. My job, along with three others, was to stick one bolt and nut in a beam where the two flanges would meet that was flown up to us and move on to the next column—we were almost running on the wet iron—to kick the next beam into place and move on. At the time I didn't think much of it. I just did what I knew I was capable of. As I reached our next tie in, Curt wasn't nowhere in sight. I called down to the crane operator and said, "Stop. Set your brake on what you have and stop."

I ran down the four-inch beam and found Curt hanging on with one hand. I was three feet away from him when his leather glove came off. I reached for him. He was gone, landing on a car on the busy street below. Utter shock. I never went to either funeral this time. I knew I would never do the job I loved again. I was sent back to Lowe's hotel. It was finished in time for the convention, before anyone else started their job for bricklayers, sheetrockers, etc.

We hung a Christmas tree atop the last piece of iron that was hung so people who drove by could see what was possible when ironworkers do their job. The people who passed by had no idea who was killed during this process. I returned to Oaklawn and Lemon. We finished it, hung a Christmas tree there as well. I stayed in this trade until I was thirty-three years old and came down, as many of you know, at my wife's request.

This story I dedicate to our daughter.

Ironworking 3

Two years have now passed since burying Curt in 1983. Four more jobs were completed, losing three more friends in that time period. On a spring morning in 1985, I couldn't sleep that night. I lay in our front lawn all night just thinking when my number was up. I went in our home, picked up a little ben wind-up clock and threw it through a window in the bedroom. Glass scattered in the lawn. Got in my 1981 short bed pickup with a 454 motor came lowered to the earth, beautiful truck with no chrome, black in color. I drove it at twenty-five years old as I do now with my 'vette.

As I pulled into our new site off central expressway on Caruth Haven Lane, three flatbed trucks were waiting to be unloaded with red iron. I walked to our trailer to sit with others before we started to unload. Mike, our union rep, was there. Mike grew up in Wyoming. James Cann, was his best friend in high school. They were bull riders. Mike pushed me to the floor as I entered the trailer. Playing wasn't playing for me.

I was pissed, broke two ribs. They wrapped me with tape, hurting bad. We unloaded the iron and set it in sequence as it would be hung. Drill trucks was there at 3:00 a.m. before anyone else to drill the piers of sixty feet deep, a casing of thirty-six inches in diameter. After drilling was completed, a day later sona tube was put in the holes to keep them from caving in. I and one other ironworker set our w40 columns in before the concrete truck arrived to fill them up with a special grade of cement. The steel that was set has to be a special grade to absorb the wind as the twenty-story building began to go up, hanging steel. Three days later more trucks had arrived with red iron.

This was going to be a Comerica bank. It's still there under another name. Many of my friends pleaded with me to go see a doctor and have my ribs wrapped the right way. I declined, told them I was fine, which I wasn't, yet I kept working. As we reached sixty feet from the ground, I slipped on some iron that was sent to us. It was coated with a poly agent to keep it from rusting in transit.

Pronounced dead on the scene. I was told they rushed me to Parkland hospital and was revived. I lay in a coma for a week. When I awoke, I jumped up in the bed and remembered saying, "Where am I?" Twenty-one ironworkers were in my hospital room. They had refused to go back to work to see if I would wake up. I never shed a tear, yet everyone else either had a lump in their throat or was crying. Two weeks later I returned to work and hung our Christmas tree atop the iron after we finished.

This is a true story I dedicate to my cousin and brother in my eyes. I was twenty-five years old. I stayed doing this job I loved for seven more years, losing, in all, thirty-one ironworking friends. Scarecrow. A three-hour write and a lifetime to live.

Justified Kill

In the summer of 1992, two sisters were born in the outskirts of San Diego, California. Lynn was the oldest by two minutes before Leslie. They grew up in a mid-class family close to the beach. Their mom and dad carried them to the ocean as toddlers. As they grew, the beach became their favorite place to hang out with their many friends.

Leslie was the wild one of the two. At sixteen years old she had become involved with some friends that were into things she had never experienced before. Two years would pass quickly. Lynn graduated with honors at Pine Hills high school while Leslie skimmed by to graduate. In 2010 Lynn entered San Diego State to study oceanography. Leslie took a job at a retail store after high school, lived with her parents, started doing speed to the point her good looks were already fading at nineteen years old. She was a mess. Her parents gave her an ultimatum to straighten up or find somewhere to live. She kept on until her parents put her clothes and belongings on the front patio of their home changed the locks. Alone and broke, she was fired from her job for failing a random drug test. With nowhere to go, she hooked with a junkie four years her senior who lived across town in a run-down home his parents had left him after they were found murdered six years earlier.

Lynn graduated from San Diego State in 2014 with her degree and pretty much lived on the ocean. The sisters tried to stay close, yet Leslie pulled away further and further until the chain was broken completely. On a foggy night on the beach in 2016, a couple was walking at the water's edge and found Leslie shot once in the head, executed at close range.

Her family was devastated. Her sister, Lynn, began to question police officers and detectives who investigated the murder with no leads to go on. Her roommate, Nick, was questioned many times. Had a solid alibi. A year would pass. Lynn never gave up hunting her sister's killer. By now the police had given up and filed Leslie's murder in the cold-case files. Lynn pleaded to reopen the case with no response. Lynn started posing as Leslie on the side of town her sister lived before her death, lost twenty pounds, wore black makeup to cover her good looks.

Six more months passed. Three a.m. on a dark street, Lynn questioned a girl who knew Leslie. She was a junkie as well as Leslie was at the time of her death. She told Lynn of a guy who might have killed her sister for not paying two thousand dollars' worth of speed. Lynn now had retribution in her eyes as her body shook. She needed a untraceable gun. She bought from the streets of San Diego, tracked down Leslie's killer, entered his place. She asked one time, "Are you Raymond?" He shook with fear as she pointed the 9 mm at him from three feet away. He answered yes in a trembling voice. With no hesitation Lynn emptied the sixteen-shot clip into his body and reentered her life back on the ocean.

Labor Day

As the days rolled by, like the seasons change, I'm reminded of how fast life ticks away. For many years I labored away not thinking of it ending as soon as it did. Nor did I realize how much I'd miss working.

The camaraderie I once had with my ironworking brothers—it still haunts me to have lost so many. They will never be forgotten, then in my later years making new friends with people I thought I'd never work with at a steel mill as a welder, then leaving there and moving on with education and becoming a chemical engineer working at a plant for eleven years. With the help of a big man from Sweden I progressed at this job easier than I could have ever imagined. He was the smart man. It took me a while to get him to say howdy to everyone, but finally it happened. I miss him. I was let go, myself and two others, in September of 2011. A new maintenance director was hired. I bounced around from job to job. Until early 2014 I resigned at a place I despised anyway, filed for my disability, denied twice, then waited nine months for a court date, a grand total of almost a three-year wait, later after going to court was awarded what was mine to begin with. It's been hard adjusting to less money. Yet it is what it is.

Now at age fifty-eight, all the knowledge I have in my head is useless. Never be to used again. I wish I could have passed more along to others the way it was passed to me. I did this when I was working and enjoyed showing new hands how to become a craftsman in all you touch. For me doing it right the first time could save your life or someone else's. It was instilled in me to do right the first time every time. I was and still am very meticulous in everything I touch. If my name is on it, when I walk away from a job, I never look back.

This is not a brag. It's a fact. Now every morning now I get up with Sherry at 4:00 a.m. and sit on the front patio and watch cars and trucks headed off to their jobs and wonder where they are going, who they work for, if they're happy with their jobs. I envy them and wish I was still working. It's in my head and heart. Yet my body doesn't cooperate like it once did. I made some very good friends through the years, hardly ever see anyone no more. For four more years I can't make a dime doing anything, or my disability disappears. Not happy with this situation. I was in the process of having a short stories book published. Now with the rules of our government, a dream until then in 2020.

I try and stay positive and look toward to the future. Having Sherry in my life makes all things possible. I dedicate this story to Jeff Standfer and my bride, Sherry Summers. Thank you to the ones who read this and understand from my perspective.

Steve "Scarecrow" Summers

License to Kill

The year is 1953. A daughter is born to Ralph and Elle Harris of Houston, Texas. They name her Justine, the year of the baby boomers. Ralph is a former WW II veteran, decorated for his heroism at the battle of Bastogne for saving four of his best friends who were hit by a mortar shell. His wife, Elle, is a doctor who graduated from the University of Kentucky. Her practice is in Houston. She is a heart specialist.

Ralph joined the FBI in 1946. He was based in Houston, yet traveled the world on special assignment. The year now is 1958. The FBI is seeking out communists across the US. Many people were falsely accused and sent to prison. The US is in chaos. Reputations are ruined.

Justine is now five years old and spends most of her days with Elle's aunt Mary. Her mom works long days. Dad is gone for most of her childhood. As time passes, Justine enters elementary school at age seven. She is a fast learner without being taught by her mom or dad. Aunt Mary becomes her only source of manners, morals, and she learns from the books she is read to at night. Her mom and dad love Justine yet are rarely around to see her grow into young adulthood.

The year is now 1968. Justine is fifteen years old. As the US grows into violence, crime, the destruction of Detroit is seen much on television and across the world. Justine entered high school and maintains a solid A plus. At her graduation in 1972, she is valedictorian. She receives a complete full-ride to any college of her choice. She chooses Harvard Law, not to become a lawyer with a hefty salary. Justine chooses criminal science behavior where she excels in four years. Her mom, dad, aunt Mary attend her graduation in 1976. Many friends and cousins also attend. She is the pride of many.

The FBI offer her a job with a team of three, Tony, Melody, and Joey. They think the world of her at first sight. She stands five feet eleven inches tall, a pure beauty. Everything about her is positive. They board their Lear jet bound for Miami to investigate a murder that has stumped local law enforcement and local FBI based in Miami for two years. When they touch down, a car is waiting to take them to their hotel. Justine is very anxious to get started on her first assignment. She doesn't unpacks but rents a car and heads straight to the FBI headquarters to retrieve all the files they have from this cold case. She is reading the file in the FBI parking lot. It's now 6:00 p.m.

She drives twenty-four miles to the crime scene, starts investigating on her own. Darkness approaches. With a flashlight, latex gloves, she begins to find two things that were missed two years earlier. She heads back to their hotel to read more of the file. As she drives, more and more things come to her about how smart this person is, reaching the hotel at 11:07 p.m.

She can't sleep. Finally at 1:00 a.m. she showers and makes her way to her bed. At 6:00 a.m. she awakens. She dresses and knocks on the doors of each of her team. They wake up, not exactly ready to go investigate. Then she waits impatiently as they get ready.

First stop, a high-end Miami club known to be owned by a notorious drug cartel. They enter with a search warrant Justine has already gotten from the night before after waking a judge in the third district of Miami. The club is closed in the early morning hours. The door is broken by a SWAT team with seven members, highly trained, ready for anything that moves. It's scary for everyone. The club is very big, covering two square blocks. No one can see, only from their flashlights.

After a complete search, one man is found in his suite inside a place where millionaires would call home. He is arrested for being in the US without papers. His name is Jose Maldonado and taken to FBI headquarters, questioned for six hours without one word coming from his mouth. He reminds them of a stone, not uttering a word. A

DNA sample is taken with his lawyer present. After three long days, the sample is returned to the team. Justine had found a cigarette butt lying more than seventy yards away and two hairs from the crime scene. She didn't say a word about it until now. A perfect match. He is transported to a local jail for processing and charged with first-degree murder.

Eleven days would pass. The team flies back to their base in Chicago where Justine is praised for her ability on her first assignment. On the twelfth day, Jose escapes with help from friends on the inside of the system that were dirty cops on his payroll, on the loose. The team flies back to Miami to help with an ongoing search. They are in Miami for thirty minutes. Justine suggests the border of Mexico, and that is exactly where they go.

As border patrol had been summoned on the day of his escape, they were looking with a full description of Jose. He was found in the flatlands on the US side by Justine and her team. He was ordered to lie down, put his hands behind his back, and lie perfectly still. The team was ten feet away when Jose rolled over and started shooting at them. Justine's forty-caliber pistol had already been drawn along with the rest of the team. The first shot hit Tony in the leg. Justine put two bullets through Jose first, one striking his heart, the second one between the eyes. DOA. Tony was treated for his wound on site, spent a week in a Miami hospital recovering, with Justine, Melody, and Joey by his side day and night, until he was ready to travel again.

This story I dedicate to my aunt Mary. A bright glowing light to anyone fortunate enough to know her. Love you.

Steve and Sherry

License to Kill

Part 2

Returning to their home base in Chicago, they are each given three days to be with their families. They say goodbye to one another, and each catch a flight home for some much-needed rest. As Justine makes her two-hour flight home to spend with Mom and Dad, she begins remembering killing Jose Maldonado and begins to cry, knowing she had done the right thing. Deep inside she was hurting for taking a human life. She had been holding back in front of her team to show them she was tough as if she had ten kills. As she exits her plane, she wipes away the tears.

Mom and dad are waiting in the luggage area. As soon as they see her, Mom realizes she is hurting. She doesn't say a word, holds her as tight as possible. They spend all three days at their beach house in Galveston, Texas, swimming, eating fresh lobster, cracked crab along with a few drinks in between. Finally Justine realizes just how hard Mom and Dad worked to put her where she is today. Aunt Mary is waiting at the beach house, surprises her with a bouquet of white roses. Justine is so happy to see her. She bursts out crying for the love, reading to her as a small child, tears of joy. Seems like in an instant she is boarding her plane back to Chicago.

It's Monday morning, another workday for her as well as her team. She greets her team in the lobby of the FBI headquarters as they get on the elevator to go to the eleventh floor to meet with Director Matt Carlson. The elevator stops on the seventh floor. Smoke filled the air with broken glass falling from the ceiling, cutting them all four up. Running out of oxygen, Tony yells "Get on the floor!" He pulls as hard as possible to open the door. After twenty minutes, they are pulled from the elevator by the Chicago fire department. Their lungs are full of smoke, immediately given oxygen and bandages for their cuts.

Melody is hurt the worst with cuts to her face and throat, bleeding badly. She is transported to a Chicago hospital from care flight to undergo immediate surgery. After six grueling days, she awakes to see her team by her side with injuries of their own. A bomb had exploded in front of the FBI building packed with enough explosives that brought down half the building on the front side, shattering windows of other high-rises for two square blocks. Cars were mangled. In all, 109 people lost their lives, including thirty-nine FBI agents, seventeen policemen, and eight firefighters and forty-five innocent people who were in the wrong place at the wrong time.

The city is in total chaos. Two teams of four are flown in from Atlanta, the other from Knoxville. Jim Bolt, a crafty old man with forty years' experience, leads the investigation, while Joey, Justine, Tony, and Melody are sent home to recover from their wounds. As Jim begins to search for clues, a fragment of the bomb is found a block away lodged in a tree. It is exotic, traceable to seller and buyer, a mistake made by Cruz Maldonado, the younger brother of Jose. Cruz is on a revenge mission for anyone connected to the murder of his brother. An all-out search is under way.

A month has now passed. Justine and her team join the search along with the Mexican SWAT team in Juarez, Mexico. Cruz is not found for many months. A one-million dollar reward is offered to anyone who knows of his whereabouts with no question asked. On a rainy day in Chicago, the phone rings at FBI headquarters. Danielle Braxton takes the call. The woman on the other end of the line speaks very little English. The call is transferred to Elliana Gomez who is fluent in five different languages. The call is traced from Tucson, Arizona. The three teams board their Lear jet to Tucson. After a search for more than three days, Cruz is caught hiding in the home of a family he has taken hostage. The teams set up around the home, evacuating the neighborhood for three miles; local police sheriff's deputies as well surround the home. Now over sixty law enforcement are in place. Jim Bolt talks through a high-volume radio from their Tahoe to release everyone in the home. After twenty-seven minutes, a seventeen-year-old young man steps outside and tells everyone "Do not shoot." He is the son of John and Anita Treadwell. He tells authorities to leave. His mom and dad are tied up and gagged, beaten from head to toe with a shotgun pointed at them, and Cruz will kill them both. His sister, Sharon, has been raped several times by Cruz. She is only fourteen years old. This infuriates everyone who hears these words coming from John Junior.

Justine is beyond words. Her blood is boiling. She is completely and utterly wanting to take Cruz out. As nightfall comes, she waits until she cannot hold her emotions back any longer. It's now 10:26 p.m. Darkness surrounds the home. She goes to one of the tahoe's, arms herself with an automatic .45 caliber machine gun, enters a full clip with three more in her right pocket. She sneaks away from everyone, goes to the back of John and Anita's home, opens a small bathroom window, and slides through with her petite body. Without making a sound, she waits till morning as the sun begins to rise so that she can see and enters the living room where Cruz is standing with shotgun in hand, now not pointing at John and Anita. The sun is blinding him from a bay window.

Justine opens fire, emptying the first clip into Cruz. He is riddled with bullets from his head and back, falls to the floor. John Junior picks up the shotgun, leans it to his head, blows hit completely from his body. Justice has now been delivered. No prison term for you, Cruz Maldonado, not wasting taxpayers' money to a life in prison.

As other officers make their way into the home, Justine is standing over him with a smile on her face. She looks down and sees his three-thousand-dollar alligator boots, gold Rolex watch. She says, "Help me drag what is left of this despicable body." They tie him to one of the FBI units, drive far out into the desert, leave him for what animal would possibly eat the rest of him, drive away. The family are given a brand-new home then asked if they wanted anything from this one.

They retrieve a few personal items. The house is then burnt to the ground. John Junior has no remorse in his part. His sister, Karen, is asked if she would like to attend counseling somewhere close by. She accepts for three months for young victims of rape. Girls and boys return home smiling and knows now she will never be on her own after making so many new friends while away.

Their new home is built within three weeks, much larger than their other one, fully furnished with clothing for all members of the family, a brand-new car with the title in hand from a local dealer. The deed of their new home is signed over to them as John Senior and Anita sit at their brand-new dining room table. The State of Arizona paid for everything. Within six months they are back on track as they were before.

If you think this is a one-time thing for families across America, you would be wrong. Good things are happening every single day. Little is ever reported by the media. All they're interested in for the most part is bad news.

Justine is given a medal from the governor of Arizona for heroism beyond the call of duty. President William H. Wyatt presents Justine with a medal that was designed by our president, made of solid gold with the inscription "Bravery," weighing at twenty-one ounces. No one else will ever receive one like this again. The mold was destroyed in a melt shop in Pittsburg, Pennsylvania, with twenty Secret Service men present.

This story I dedicate to my beautiful and wonderful aunt Mary. To know her is to love her. We will forever love you.

Steve and Sherry Summers

Lightning Bolt

Lightning can strike any place it desires. For two small boys it struck within ten feet of them. We clasped our hands together and took off running until our hearts were beating a mile a minute, falling down in an old lady's front yard. She came out carrying on with us for being in her yard. We laughed at the old wench and walked away. Never in our lives had we seen it up close as much as that day.

Finding a friend who was from the same state that I was born in was something to process. Wayne was born in Kentucky like I was and moved to Kopperston, West Virginia, close to the same time as I did. A friendship started immediately. I loved his mom and dad as he did mine. We ran in and out of each other's houses, always letting the screen doors slam behind us. We were good kids, just mischievous. Wayne's dad was always working on an old Pontiac. So automatically we became Pontiac fans. There was only one year between us. I was born on October 10, 1957, and Wayne on October 10, 1958. We went through Kopperston without a care. Everyone looked after each other there, a great place to grow up in. Not many places were like Kopperston, which made a good feeling for all. As we grew, we went through the bicycle stage, then minibikes with gasoline motors, no more peddling we loved that. Cars were what we wanted next.

One day when I was in the post office I ran into Jimmy Ford. He had a '69 GTO parked across the road from his house. A snow plow had hit the rear quarter panel and damaged it some. By then he had bought a '69 Cross Ram Camaro I asked him if he would sell the GTO. He said yes, but he said it needed a transmission. I bought the GTO for fifty dollars and pulled it home after digging all the snow away from it. Only fifty-six thousand miles. My cousin Billy helped me and Dad change the transmission, and I had wheels, and it would fly. Wayne's dad had built him a Pontiac Firebird. It was a good-looking car that would run.

Now I'm eighteen years old, and Wayne is seventeen years old. We gathered a lot at Rick's drive-in and played foozball and pin ball. A few were headed to Crouch's farm to party. I asked Wayne to follow us down. Wayne declined, said he's going over to his girlfriend's house, Cathy Combs, then going our separate ways. The party broke up late that night, and I started home. As I reached a straight stretch near Kopperston across Henry Pruetts Gulf gas station, I came up on a wrecker and Wayne's car wrapped around a tree near the creek.

I hoped for the best and got the worst at seventeen. Wayne lost his life that night. I don't remember driving the rest of the way home. I went in the back door and heard the screen door slam like I had many times before, lay in my daddy's lap and cried and cried. Dad had already heard and was waiting on me. From the night Wayne died, not many days go by I don't think of him. To know Wayne was to love him.

My Earliest Years Growing Up in Kentucky

I was born to Clarence Steven Summers Sr. and Wanda Lucille Oakley Summers. I was given his name, Clarence Steven Summers Jr., tipping the scales at nine pounds and fourteen ounces. One of my earliest memories was taking a bath in a wash tub at my granny Oakley's house with boiled water from the stove. She had no indoor plumbing at this time. Going to the outhouse in the winter months was a quick trip for me. A old Sears catalog was a source for cleaning yourself.

A warm morning coal-burning stove was her heating for the whole house. I remember going to the coal house, which most everyone had, and shoving coal in a coal bucket, wading through snow almost as tall as I was to keep the fire going in a two-story house. My granny loved RC cola. Sometimes I would try and sneak one to drink. Always getting caught. She always greeted me with a big, sloppy kiss, without her teeth. In seems I was forever wiping slobbers off my cheeks with my shirtsleeve, yet I loved her more than I can express.

As far I as I can remember, we had indoor plumbing at our house, which I loved. At four years old a big truck-like van would come around and sell candy and popsicles, plus fresh vegetables. Mom would give me a nickel for a banana popsicle, a highlight for my day. Then as I came off the truck one day, a '58 Chevrolet Biscayne ran over me. My cousin Billy Summers was with me. He ran to Mom to tell her what had happened. I was taken to the clinic where I was born. Then my dad left work to come see me thinking the worst. There were tire tracks on both my legs, cut up and bruised with no broken bones. Even the doctor could not believe nothing was broke on my legs. A few days later I was running and jumping like nothing ever happened.

Mom had seven brothers, and I thought they hung the moon. They would take me shooting a .22 rifle. Skinny-dipping in a nearby stream you could drink the water, and we did many times. Many of them are gone now, yet I remember each and every one of them. They loved me, and I loved them. An old man, I remember his name was Pizanna, an Italian man with care worn face with dirty beige pants on and an opened shirt, which was tucked in. He had a way about him I loved. I was six years old. He said all the time, "Hotta-mighty 7," and I repeated it many times, but not in front of my mom. Only once did I do this in front of her. Yet I kept saying it to everyone else.

The mountain you came off to reach Lynch was called Black Mountain. At the very tip of the mountain you could put one foot in Virginia and the other in Kentucky, which I did as a small boy when my uncles were with me. My grandpa Oakley we called Poppie, a very quiet man who had lost a leg in the coal mines in his early years. He then went on to become a preacher, bloody Harlan, as it was known back in the 1920s when the union came in to make it a safer and better place for the men who worked in the worst of conditions, finally winning over the coal companies who owned the mines, to make what was bad better.

When Dad was laid off from US Steel, I was crushed, knowing we were moving to West Virginia. My cousins Greg, Valerie, and all my Summers cousins I would be leaving at seven years old. Not knowing any other life but my home was never to be again. I often wonder what my life would have been like if we had never moved, yet I would have never met Sherry, the love of my life. So looking back I'm happy we did. In the early 2000, thousands on a trip to see Mom. We went back to Lynch and Cumberland, a small town six miles from Lynch, and then on to Harlan to see more family I hadn't seen in years. We stopped where I was born, which was closed except for a small clinic. A nurse there gave us a guided tour of the old hospital. In the ruins of what once was, Mom showed me exactly where I was born, a trip back in time I'll forever remember.

For the ones who may read this, please go back to the song I posted with Patty Loveless. This may make you understand more of where I came from! For those of you that have been to Gary, West Virginia, the houses there look the same as they did in Lynch. Thank you all for listening.

Steve

On My Own

On a cold rainy morning at 4:38 a.m. just south of Portland, Oregon, cries come out from Cynthia Hammond. Her husband, Bill, quickly awakens. He knows it's time for their first child to be born. Living in an upscale neighborhood, it's not far to the hospital. When they arrive at the ER, she is wheeled to the maternity ward. At 6:17 a.m., their son is born. A name was already thought through and given to him, Nate. He will be their only child.

As he grows, he develops the love for sports and girls. Baseball is his favorite, yet he's good in all, little league, high school baseball, and finally college, graduating with a degree in architectural engineering, lands a job with a major firm in Clearwater, Florida. After many firms interviewed him, he chose Florida—women, fast cars, and bars. Nate was excellent at what he did and loved doing it.

Now twenty-six years old, he was independent and loved his freedom, owned his own condo. Nate had reached a goal some never do, designing buildings all over the world, bought a '69 Chevelle 396 engine, four-speed beautiful jet black with black interior, his pride and joy. Nate dated a lot of women his age and some older but not attached to anyone. He was enjoying life.

The perfect job, more money in the bank than you or I could imagine. On a long weekend he was out with friends drinking at the local bars. It started getting late. So he started home at 3:00 a.m. weaving with too much alcohol in him, driving too fast at 115 miles an hour, slid off the two-lane highway, thrown from the car.

At 6:17 a.m. a man going to work saw the Chevelle wrapped around a tree with no one inside, only blood. He was frantic, trying to find the driver. Sixty feet away Nate was lying in a ditch covered in blood. He called the police and paramedics. Nate was breathing but not by much, rushed to the trauma unit in Miami by helicopter with many life-threating injuries, a broken leg, severe fracture, a hole in his lower stomach, losing his left arm, which was found and reattached, one punctured lung, head trauma, deep cuts and bruising covering his twenty-six-year-old body.

Nate's parents were notified and not given any information until they arrived in Miami the following day. Three trauma surgeons worked on Nate for seventeen hours with little hope given to his parents. Nate lay in a coma for eleven months. The doctors advised his parents to turn off the machines that were keeping his body alive. His mom and dad wouldn't do it or talk to the doctors about this. Over two thousand family and friends visited him while he lay there in a coma.

At 4:38 on a Sunday morning, Nate awoke to find his parents and a nurse who had cared for him. Her name was Shelly around Nate's age. She had fallen in love with him while caring for him in the coma ward, changing his IVs, cleaning him daily, Nate not knowing he had someone doing all these things that needed done on a daily basis. He was released from the hospital two months later. His job was still waiting. He returned to work and married Shelly one year later, a small ceremony with a thousand family and friends. Now thirty-six years old, they have two children, a boy and a girl. Shelly still works in the coma ward. Nate has become the general manager of the firm in Clearwater. Nowadays Nate drives a Nissan Quest minivan to carry his children back and forth to their soccer games and baseball of course, but never lost his love for cars. He now also engineers cars for drag racing and Nascar.

Thank y'all for reading this.

Steve "Scarecrow" Summers

Outlaw Man

On April seventh in the year of 1867, Sam and I were riding in one of the worst dust storms we'd ever seen. Entering the Oklahoma Territory, we came upon a little town and stopped to have a drink of whiskey. Our horses were worn out and so were we. After we went to have our horses watered and fed, we saw a saloon, went in for a glass of whiskey. We saw three card games being played by drovers and ranch hands. We approached a table and sat down, dealt in right away.

A barmaid came by and asked if anyone needed anything. Guy spoke up, said, "Bring me and my friend a bottle." The game was going well. We were winning a little money between us, which was very much needed. One hour went by. I noticed one of the drovers slipping cards from beneath his sleeve. With no hesitation I stood up, drew my .45 Colt, shot and killed him. Guy then stood as well, pulled his .45 Smith and Wesson, pointed it at the barkeep who had pulled a shotgun from beneath the bar, shot and killed him. We held our pistols at the other men at the table.

I grabbed the money that was on the table. We backed out slowly, walked to the livery stable, got our horses, and rode hard out this chicken shit town. On the run, we were caught entering Kansas by a posse who had been chasing us for miles, remained in a small prison for seven years. We escaped after spending two years in that dirt floor cell and rode harder than ever, stopping when we had to resupply for ourselves plus our horses. Two years would pass.

As we entered Kentucky, it was cold and snowing. Came across a wagon train stuck in the heavy snow in the Blue Ridge Mountains. We helped them get moving and became good friend with over fifty of them, headed to land that was not claimed. We both took a wife at age thirty and settled in the flat lands of Virginia where no one knew of our past and what we had done in our early years. Even today we still talk about our outlaw days and smile, knowing we're safe. Guy and his wife Jesse had three children. I and Rebecca Lynn had two children, lived out the rest of our days reminiscing of days gone by.

This story I dedicate to my best friend.

The Oxbow

As I began to pack my truck, the rain started pouring. I came in and changed clothes and waited for the rain to stop finally, ready to leave. Sherry was very apprehensive about me going alone, yet I did— smooth driving until I came into Amarillo. Sleet and ice covered the road. I drove on a lot slower, which was very aggravating. Twenty-four hours later I found myself in Oxbow County, Montana. Found a small motel, got me something to eat, and fell asleep across the bed. The next morning I went down to a local stable and rented a mountain horse and a pack mule, three hours later packed and ready to ride.

The first two hundred yards was flat land and then the incline started. After riding for eight hours, I stopped and set up camp for the night. It was peaceful. Built myself a fire, fed the horse and mule, watered them down as well, then fed myself. It was cold, like I'd never been before, crawled in my goose down sleeping bag and listened to the firewood pop, a sound I hadn't heard since leaving West Virginia.

The morning sun awoke me the next day, bit off some beef jerky, got ready and started what I was hoping would be my last day to the top. It was not to be. The snow started falling to almost a whiteout, found shelter in a cave. I, the horse, and pack mule waited it out. Two days later the snow was up to my knees. Now losing time and running low on supplies, I made my way out and began again. Two thousand feet to the top of the ridge where the Indians lived in their old ways. Having Blackfoot blood in me, I had to see where they once lived. After pulling the horse and mule finally to the top, I was there. We rested for a while and set up camp. I tied the mule up.

I and the horse began to explore. After about a mile ride, I came upon a teepee. It was empty, yet you could tell someone lived there. I pulled my 30/30 rifle and walked around looking for anyone who was still living. Inside the teepee was a bow and arrows from the late 1800s, Indian clothing not from today's cultures. Then an old Sioux Indian appeared. We looked at each other like is this happening or not. There was a language barrier. I didn't speak Sioux, and he didn't speak Blackfoot. He motioned for me to come into his home. I was reluctant but went anyway.

He cooked some deer meat. We ate. Traded my 30/30 for his bow and arrows. Then after the trade we said our goodbyes the best we could, and I left. The next morning I packed what supplies I had, left, and began my descent back down the ridge, covering a little over four thousand feet in a week and three days, now heading home looking forward to seeing Sherry.

I arrived home eighteen hours after, leaving the Oxbow, much better driving conditions. I carried the bow and arrows to have them appraised. The bow was worth seven thousand dollars, and the seven arrows one thousand dollars apiece.

I will never part with any of them, part of my heritage! Sincerely, Steve "Scarecrow" Summers.

Persecuted

A story of the Indians who once roamed this land in peace and prosperity, forming tribes and living in peace for the most part. They hunted and killed what they only needed to survive. They loved their families and prayed to God. When killing a buffalo, every part was used for meat to feed themselves and clothing also for warming in the winters on the Great Plains—a life for them that would end in 1492 when the Europeans landed on their land.

After this wars broke out between the Indians and the Europeans, forced from their land. Many Indians migrated to the western part of their country to get away from fighting and live in peace. Over one hundred years later, the British and French fought over Indian land, making a country that didn't belong to either of them. The British won this war against the French and drove them back to France. Now the British thought this was their land. Wrong in my eyes. Still and will always be Indian land.

In 1830 Andrew Jackson set an act in motion to drive the Indians out of their country to only live on reservations and receive rations from the American government. Indians did not like their way of life and fought back only to be killed, their women raped; children were killed as well by the Yankee blue coats. Settlers moved west. I will admit some were killed by some tribes, an act of protecting their land. This wasn't the settlers' land to begin with. Trappers also moved west, only to kill the buffalo and skin them, leaving the meat to rot in the sun. A disgrace for all who have Indian blood running through their veins.

This country, now called America, is not America at all the way I see it. Some Indians today still live on reservations. Pride we once held is now a fading memory in most Indians. I am ashamed of this country for what has happened. There is no changing what has happened. We are a long-forgotten people who once lived on our own land. I wear a necklace made from my people of an Indian feather that I love, handmade, also a ring made from real silver, shale, turquoise, and coral. I did not mention the steel rail that went through our land.

This story is a shorter version. Many more facts could have been written, yet I will end it here. I dedicate this story to Melinda Cook for inspiring it to be written from a post I saw of hers. We both share a common interest in our great heritage and all who carry Indian blood.

Premonitions

In the summer of 1990 miners' vacation, my mom and dad drove to Texas for a two-week visit. Sherry and I, as always, were excited to see them. We lived out in the country on Farm Road 1446, an eighty-acre farm with two horses, a large barn, pecan trees, two ponds—a dream home for us we never expected to call our own. In 1991 it all came crashing down as the government decided to build a nuclear collider. We were displaced. Since that day, I have despised the government and continues today.

I had made horseshoe pits and filled them with sand a few yards from our home. My dad taught me how to play horseshoes at a very young age. In time I got better until Dad couldn't beat me no more. As we played in the shade of two big oak trees, walking back and forth to see who was the closest, in no less than a horseshoe width away he had beaten me. I was thinking, "How did that happen," LOL. He looked directly at me and said, "Steve, did you let me win?" I said, "Absolutely not," remembering vividly he was almost running into our home to tell Mom, Sherry, Jessica, and two-year-old Jacob he had finally beat me. I was so happy for him.

While they were there, we traveled to Mesquite to see the rodeo with bull riders, also went to the lake in Waxahachie, went downtown to the county courthouse, which is known as the most beautiful in Texas. The two weeks flew by. As they had done every year they came, Dad and I made plans to go to South Padre the following summer to go deep-sea fishing on a charter boat. We were both excited more than I can tell you. I told when y'all come next summer I'll have a new engine in my 1977 GMC pickup and one thousand dollars in cash. The plan was set.

On a Saturday, the day they were getting ready to leave, Dad walked through every room of our home looking around like he knew something I had no clue of. When we reached the bedroom Mom and him had slept, he stopped and told me, "Steve, you know if I die my model '97 Winchester twelve-gauge shotgun is yours." I had known this for years. I was puzzled to say the least. As we walked out onto the front patio, I stopped. I could never walk him to their car. He turned. Big tears welled up in my eyes as did his. I remember waving from the patio as they drove away.

Sherry and Jessica knew to leave me alone for the rest of that day. I went out near the horseshoe pits and got into Jessica's tire swing I had made for her and just wept for hours. Later that evening about dark, I went into our home. No one said a word to me, for they knew where my heart was. It had left with him. On a perfect day on October 30, I was at work running a 3900 Manitowoc crane. This was a job I took to save Sherry's sanity from being an ironworker. Before leaving Chaparral Steel, I self-taught myself to run 988 loaders. Any piece of heavy equipment I could run and loved doing it to break up the monotony of being stuck in my welding bay day after day. It was a slow day, the reason I was running the crane. I was caught up in all my welding duties. We were in the direct flight line of the geese flying south for the winter. Thousands were above. As I watched, I was in awe at their perfect flight alignment. Three-thirty came, time to drive that thirteen-mile trip home. I was ready.

I pulled into our driveway on Crown Over Road. Sherry was standing on the steps of our patio as I turned the old truck off. She said in a trembling voice, "You need to come in." I remember saying, "Let me check my oil first, the motor is getting worse." "Please," she said, "now." So I walked in. Sherry said, "Sit down, I have something to tell you.", I eagerly awaited. She broke the news Dad had passed away due to a massive heart attack. I was in disbelief at first then started crying uncontrollably.

Even today twenty-nine years later, Sherry still says that was hardest thing she has ever done. It all happened so fast. Only my brother and sister, and I flew to Charleston to be picked up by some church friends of theirs. I never once removed my sunglasses on the flight or in the van. We were brought to what was Mom's home. I was in pieces. As hard as I tried, I could not pull myself together.

He was buried in Rockwood, Tennessee, his place of birth, born December 4, 1926. My cousin Billy saved what sanity I had left by riding with him to Tennessee. The service was held at Toneda Baptist Church.

I remember Debbie singing with her beautiful voice at his funeral. Jess Brunty, Lisa dad, came. As I saw him walk up the concrete steps of Toneda, I felt some relief. He was a good man. I remember when Jess passed my heart sank. Returning home three days later, I was no better than before. I couldn't go to work for two weeks. My boss Jim Carroll kept calling, pleading for me to come to work. He said it would help. On the second day of the third week I returned with nothing to say to anyone.

Exactly one year later I had replaced the motor in my old truck, had my thousand dollars like I said I would. I remember Carl coming over on the anniversary of his passing while I was changing my oil. As he drove up, I crawled out from underneath. I looked into his eyes, trying so hard to put the words together: "My truck is ready, I have my money, I just don't have a dad to go fishing with." We hugged as the tears fell from both our eyes. For months after retiring walking to the post office every day it was open, his black lung came. Three days after he was gone from this earth.

Something I thought I would never write has now been written. Honestly I did cry while writing. To this day I was never told by anyone what time he passed. I told my brother and two sisters, "If you ever tell me, I will disown you."

There were many other things that was said by Dad that was so out of character for him to say. Before he passed, he told the preacher at Toneda, "You fed my soul with your sermon." In all the years we went to church, I had never heard him utter anything of the sort. Deep in my heart I really think he knew the end was soon as it came to pass. He never met a stranger, mild-mannered, with a heart of gold.

I started this story Tuesday night, which was the day Dad passed on, and wrote through the night. It is now four minutes after 4:00 a.m. As I close eight hours later, Wednesday morning, I hope to get some sleep today as my eyes are still glued wide open, I dedicate this true story to everyone who had a loving dad like mine. A small footnote: Sherry lost her dad at ten months old. He got to know Sherry. When she was only fifteen years old, her mom, Casperetta, would let her come to our home in Kopperston and play cards. Canasta, most of the time, was the game we played. My dad loved her as he did his own children. To know him was to love him.

Pug

A few words before I begin to write this story of my friend, now gone from this earth for more than twenty-five years, yesterday around 4:00 p.m., Sherry put me in a place called Wordpad where you can write at your leisure and not be interrupted. At 6:00 p.m. I looked at the screen. Not a word had been written. By 9:30 p.m., still nothing.

What I want you to try and understand is how hard it is to write this story, about James PUG Elswick and the one I write in October is of Wayne Newsome. Wrap yourself in this with me, and I hope you realize what it means to me and how much I miss and love both these fine young men. It is now 2:30 a.m. June 3. I awoke much earlier than usual. James was all I could think about. My hope is you understand what I'm trying to say. Some may ask why I put myself through this. That's a question even I can't answer, yet I wouldn't have it any other way. It's now 4:30 a.m., and I will take a break and return later on to finish—in between the hours that pass without writing much at all.

I think of his sons and grandchildren and what they are missing in a man they would have loved beyond imagination. It is now 3:00 p.m. in the afternoon. Once again I hope to complete my story of James. Thank you for your patience.

The story of James "Pug" Elswick. After moving from Kentucky to West Virginia at seven years old, James, Tim, Tommy, and Guy, Mike, Wayne Newsome, and of course the Cassell clan were some of the first friends I made, and they were good ones. James had a charismatic smile like few I'd ever seen. From day one we were attached at the hip—shooting marbles, playing in the dirt, swimming in the creek, walking the railroad tracks. All things little boys do together. As we grew bicycles were bought for us by our parents. We rode to the Kopperston Tipple and farther, and none of us was supposed to be on the road (smiling).

Our baseball team was the best, the Cardinals, coached by James's dad, Pug Senior. Making it to the all-star games was the thrill of a lifetime, then came minibikes. LOL. That was a mistake by our parents. A gasoline engine. Boy howdy. In heaven.

These memories flow like blood through my veins. Forever remembered, never to be washed away. There is so much to write of James. The mischievous acts I'll leave out. My friend and I would like to avoid prosecution. Not sure what the statute of limitations are (LOL). In Kopperston there was an ongoing argument about which camp was the best. The upper or the lower. For the people who lived in the upper camp it was the best. Since I lived there, it was the best (LOL). people in the lower camp thought theirs was the best. All in all they were both great places to grow up in.

James would have been fifty-seven years old today. I will always miss him and love him as a friend that compares to none. For over twenty years I called his mom on his birthday. With Hazel's passing, I now call his sister.

I will close for now. Anyone who read this are more than welcome to leave a comment of a memory you have of James. Today was hard and will continue to be. I doubt that I will answer anyone's comment. For I'm beyond any more words! A song will follow this story later, his favorite song by Loggins and Messina. Thank y'all.

Steve

Rain

As a seven-year-old boy peers through a dirty wooden frame window in a rent house, he is unsure of his surroundings. His older brother and baby sister look on as the rain pours down. For three days and nights the rain never stops. He tries to amuse himself in a place he has never lived before and knows no one. Feeling lost and alone he doesn't like where his parents have moved them to. All he can think about is the home where he has left his friends and cousins. For now he is totally lost. It is a unbearable, three days for him and his older brother. This little boy was me, first three days in Kopperston. This story is inspired by a rainy day in Texas.

Remembering Friends

On June 3, 1958, a son was born to Hazel "Sexton" Elswick and James Elswick with a sparkle in his eye and a smile that was like no other. He would be named James after his dad. James was the third child born to the Elswicks. Two sisters, Patricia and Debbie. As he grew, you could tell he was going to be a very good athlete. I first met James when we moved from Kentucky to Kopperston when I was seven and he was six. We became inseparable, did everything together, rode our bikes, played marbles, played catch as kids. We even swam in the creek across from our houses.

In the fall after the leaves had fallen, we would go to the back of the island creek store and get cardboard that appliances had come with, climb up the side of the mountains. Once reaching as far as we could go, we'd fold the cardboard over our feet and slide back down faster than a bullet, dodging trees when possible, though we hit a few, laughed, got back on, and slid as far as we could.

The winter months in Kopperston were cold and snow covered. Sleigh-riding time if you were fortunate enough to have one. We used cardboard for the years we didn't have one, some of the most memorable times of our lives. There were so many things we did with Tim, Tommy r, Guy, and others. In our early teens, we would ride our bikes to the rec building and coast back to the island creek store. None of us was supposed to ride on the main road, but we did, LOL. Competition was big between us all. Whoever got there first was the winner.

We played flys and first bouncers, basketball at the tennis court below our school. I still have the basketball we used most times, not a grip left on. It's slick as Reece Pennington's head. He was a grump.

Now a little older, our parents made a huge mistake in buying us minibikes—gasoline power—no more pedaling. We were the terror of the upper camp and loved for all who suffered from it.

Wayne hit a car once, backing out of an alley, threw him over the car, and he landed in a sticker bush. The rest of us barely got stopped. After seeing Wayne was okay, we laughed at him so hard. Then we all rode on. I could go on and on about James. One more thing, his dad was our baseball coach in little league. We beat every team my last year. Then I was too old. It was one of the best teams I'd ever played with. That year we won the all-star game with James pitching. He had a great curve ball.

As time passed, I married and moved to Texas in 1981. James stayed and became a coal miner. I wanted no part of the mines. We stayed in touch by telephone and talked about all fun we had growing up in a great neighborhood. Kopperston ended up being a safe and desirable place to live in the sixties and seventies. On March 1, 1988, our son was born. James called to congratulate us.

James had been battling leukemia for quite a few years, I kept up with his ups and downs. In September of 1988, I called him to check on how he was doing. He said he was okay, but I read through the lines and knew better. I told him we were leaving for Padre Island for a few days to enjoy the beach and asked him if he would be okay while we were gone. He said, "Sure, call me when you get back." Little did I know James would pass away while we were gone. My dad called and told me of his passing. I was beside myself with remorse that I wasn't there. To this very day my heart weeps for him. Changed my life forever. He was planning a trip to Texas in the spring of 1989. To know him was to love him. The smile he had I'll carry with me until I leave this earth.

Thank you for all who read this. It was a pleasure to write up until the ending. Thank you.

Steve Summers

A Rite of Passage

My career started in high school taking welding classes, not what my mom and dad wanted for me. I had a chance to go to Marshall university and run track with a scholarship that they had offered and learn to become an x-ray technician. It was not to be. I didn't want anything more to do with school. In hindsight, so wrong was I. In 1977 I landed a job in the union working on a new coal preparation plant being built in Sabine, West Virginia. Thinking I knew everything about welding, I found quickly I knew nothing.

So I was taught by men at the age I am now and younger. After working there for almost two years, I learned so much about my trade. While there I was more interested in becoming an ironworker, which I did. Starting on the bolt up crew, heights never bother me. So this came natural. One day I went over and sat down with three people. They asked, "What do you think you're doing?" I answered, "Having lunch with you guys." I was told I hadn't earned my keep enough to eat with them. Not understanding I moved on to another place to eat.

Soon the coal industry fell on hard times, moved on to Texas where home was for us anyway. Joining the union in Fort Worth, very quickly moving up the ranks to a connectors job in five short years. This was where the action was for me. I loved being five hundred to eight hundred feet in the free open air. The summer months were worse than winter months, average tool belt weight forty-five to sixty pounds. I had cut me a piece of plywood ten inches by ten, hooked it to my tool belt with jack chain for sitting on the steel. Reaching temperatures of 140 degrees, you had to have something to sit on while sticking a bolt through a beam and then moving on to your next tie in.

In the winter months I have blown ice from a beam with a cutting torch to get across to the next tie in. Once a young buck came and sat with us to enjoy his lunch and hear our stories of jobs we've been on and finished. He was told like I was years earlier to move on. Men were lost, I knew, and called more than friends. We were brothers with not knowing what fear was. We had painted on our hard hats a No Fear logo, two feathers. A young man with talents you would not believe painted this logo on our hard hats. I lost him to an operation's error. It took three men to pull us from his beaten body when the dust settled. In all I lost seven of the best men anyone could call a brother. The graphic details are left out for the ones who may read this.

I never thought I would give up what I loved doing. Yet I did in 1987 when I learned Sherry was pregnant with Jake. This was the turning point for me to move on to a safer environment for my family. This untold story is something I've never shared with anyone. Until now—God bless.

This story I dedicate to my wife, Sherry Summers, for accepting me as I was then and am today.

Runaway

Lilly Keller was born in the woodlands, a suburb of Houston, Texas, on November 23, 2000, a beautiful young girl with an Asian mother and white father. Lilly was a cheerleader with a heart of gold to everyone she came to know. Her parents were very strict yet caring of her. She stood five feet nine inches tall, long flowing jet-black hair. What I would call perfection.

One day after school she never showed up for cheerleading practice. Her friends were concerned about her whereabouts. A good girlfriend of hers called Lilly's cell phone. No answer. Then she called Lilly's mom and dad. An all-out search for her began with no clues to go on.

Lilly had ran away—picked up on the road out of the woodlands to somewhere, anywhere but home. She was tired of being ruled by her parents. A month would pass. The community raised a fifty-thousand-dollar reward for her return to no avail. Six months later she was sold and bought to the Russian mafia from our own government to be whored out to men with lots of money. Lilly was beaten and raped by her pimp because she didn't like what was going on in her new life.

One year later everyone who had looked for her had given up, except her mom and dad. On a cold night in Chicago, Lilly was sent to a man's home for 1,500 hundred dollars a night. She told him what had happened to her. He did not care, just wanted sex with Lilly, which she had to do, not willingly. Three more months would pass. Many others had their way with her. In the spring she was sent back to the very same man with the big home and plenty of money.

She pleaded again ("Please help me."). This man had grown a conscience and let her call her mom and dad from his home. The Chicago PD was called in, and Lilly explained to them what had happened. One senator and three congressmen were arrested for trafficking young girls from all over the United States and sold to different organizations across America and many foreign countries. Lilly was flown home to Houston where her parents and over seven hundred friends were waiting for her plane to land. As Lilly came down the steps of the Lear jet, a roar like you've never heard embraced her, reunited with her mom and dad in a limo the rich man provided.

Two days later a parade was given for Lilly's return in her hometown, invited were many more from our government. Three from the Russian mafia were found dead in Chicago with more leads pouring in from other young girls all over the world who were released.

Thank y'all for reading.

Scarecrow

Saran Wrap

In the winter of 1977 in Sabine, West Virginia, I was working as an ironworker welder at a very young age. Sherry and I had only been married for a short time, and Sherry was pregnant with our first child, Jessica. We were living in a single wide trailer on Groush's farm. Jess Brunty and Dollie, his wife, owned the property with his children, two adorable girls. All we owned was a nineteen-inch Magnavox TV we had bought from Bob Fields in Oceana at an appliance store and Corelle dishes plus silverware.

The trailer was partially furnished. Jess was one of the best men I've ever known. On a very cold morning, driving on a snow-covered road in our '69 GTO, I made it to work fine. I drove up and parked. I saw Sam r coming out of the company trailer of Roberts and Schaffer. We spoke, and he told me go and start making up bolts with four other ironworkers. A coal preparation was being built. Everyone else had been sent home due to the snow and cold that morning. It was twenty-three degrees. Four hours passed for this. We would be paid eight hours.

Sam was the safety director and a good one. He walked up to us and asked if anyone wanted to stay and weld a broken pipe. No one uttered a word. Seemed like a lifetime passed and then I said I'll do it. First, I walked with Sam to the first-aid station. I wasn't sure what I had gotten myself into. As two men started wrapping me in saran wrap, I knew exactly what needed done. They wrapped me in so many layers I could barely walk. Duct tape was used to secure my hands so I could wear my leather gloves.

A concrete tunnel on a slope was flooded with water. Pumps were frozen so the water could not be pumped out. I had my welding hood on, which I kept through the years as a reminder of that day. Holding five 6010 welding rods between my teeth, I started my descent down the tunnel. As the water rose around, I hoped there were no tears in my welding lead, which I carried over my shoulder, for if there was, it would have shocked me. Now I reach the broken pipe that was anchored to the side of the tunnel.

I told Sam I was fine and began to weld the pipe. Standing in freezing water that was up to my collarbones, I was shaking so bad. I pulled a welding rod from my teeth with my right hand and made my first weld. I could barely see the pipe except when I struck an arc. It was dark in the tunnel like a dungeon. As I pulled my second welding rod from my teeth, I lost my right glove in the water. My hand was wet from feeling around to try and find it, never did. As I made my second pass around the pipe, I was getting lit up from electricity from my welder. I made one more pass. Now I'm almost getting knocked down in the water. I screamed to the top and said, "Try it and we'll see if it leaks." I had one drip from the pipe. Sam screamed to me get out of there now. I didn't. I screamed back to Sam, "When I tell you to kill the welder, turn it off."

Lord this last time when I struck an arc it blew me under the water. I came up out of the water screaming "Turn the welder the hell off." I threw the lead to the water, threw my hood off, and started running as fast as I could to be free from the water. As I made my way out, three men were standing there to free me from the saran wrap. I was frozen, literally frozen. They carried me to the first-aid station and covered me with blankets to warm my skin. I couldn't feel anything.

Three hours passed. I started feeling some warmth. Sam called an ambulance. I wouldn't go. This was on a Tuesday. I drove home in only a blanket. The next day I went to work. Sam was standing at the gate, stopped me and said, "Go home, Steve." I said, "Why?" "Because I said so." They paid me triple time through the rest of the week including Saturday and Sunday. Monday when I parked my car, Sam came out and said, "That is the bravest thing I've ever seen in my life." I smiled and walked away smiling all the way to meet up with my fellow ironworkers.

This is a true story. Looking back now, I would have done it all over again.

Scarecrow Steve Summers

Sardines and Jell-O

As far as I can remember, I shared a post of my health a few months ago, which was a good report. As I entered my doctor's office I smelled the most awful smell in my life. I walked to the receptionist. She was eating sardines, a young girl that is the nurse's daughter. You can have a prescription called in from a pharmacy. Days will go by and no response, which burns me up. I need my pills, like everyone one else.

My good friend for over thirty years once worked for my doctor and is now a dental assistant with my dentist. A few days later I had an appointment with my dentist. I was telling her what happened at my doctor's office. She started laughing uncontrollably for minutes. She was in tears laughing so hard.

A week passed. I was in a grocery store buying a few items, just happened to see a can of sardines. My mind went to work, so I bought them. Three days passed. As I entered my dentist's office I had them concealed in my front pocket. Five minutes later I was called in. Le Ann met me at the door. I was seated in the dentist's chair. As they started lean the chair back, I said, "Wait, I have something for you." I pulled the sardines from my pocket and handed them to her. Again she was laughing very hard.

Two weeks passed. I went for another appointment. By now everyone that worked in the office had heard of what I did. I walked up to the front desk and said, "I'm Steve Summers, I have an appointment at 2:00 p.m." She was smiling, got me to thinking, "What's going on?" When I met Lee Ann, she was holding a plate full of Jell-O with the can of sardines in the middle of the Jell-O.

The worm had turned on me. Now I was set up. She and most of the staff were laughing as she handed me the plate. Being myself I just laughed it off, and we had a picture made from my camera I just happened to have along with me.

There will be times the joke is on us when we think we are going to be the funny one with the last laugh. Sometimes think again. This story I dedicated to my dad who was also a joker. Through the years I have become more like him than I could have ever imagined. Very happy things worked out that I am!

Serial Killer

Part one

On the back roads of northern Idaho, two miles from the pavement on a dirt road, live Merle and Dixie McBride. Merle is a second-generation dirt farmer and not much of one. He has been arrested for many petty crimes, most recently the beating of his wife, and many were never reported. Dixie stays. She has nowhere else to go. They live in a run-down shack with no heating except a fireplace, no air-conditioning, only a mattress on the floor to sleep on, no running water, just a well on a cold night—it dips into the low twenties.

In 1965 in November, Dixie gives birth to a son at home. She was a nursing aid before marrying. Merle is off drinking somewhere on what little money they have. He is reckless and mean. He has no friends whatsoever. As he returns home, he is pissed even though he knew Dixie was pregnant. Little baby Ronnie has no idea what his future will bring. Soon to find out his dad was throwing Ronnie up against the wall at three years old, at five years old working in the fields being cussed, Merle saying "Can't you do nothing right!"

By the time he reached puberty, Merle was making him have sex with his own wife, Dixie, and laughing as he watched. Dixie was horrified but couldn't say a word. Finally at age eighteen Ronnie walked down the two-mile dirt road to the pavement and hitched a ride with no education and only the clothes on his back. After two days of countless rides, he was in Boise, Idaho. First, he robs a Stop and Go. With four hundred dollars to his name, next he steals a car and heads north to Wyoming.

Running low on money he breaks into a home in a rural neighborhood. As he broke the glass in a window, a dog begins to bark. He makes his way in. Husband and wife are asleep. He first slides a knife into the husband's throat. He is dead in less than a minute. He ties the wife up and starts making her do sexual things to him, rapes her, sodomizes her, slit her throat. He leaves through the front door, taking all their jewelry and money. Back on the road he heads south to Amarillo, Texas, stops at a rich couple's home, breaks through a side window once again. As the owner approaches Ronnie, he punches him and knocks him out, ties him up in the closet in their bedroom and hangs him to an overhanging rafter, then begins raping his wife then stabs her thirty-three times.

For Ronnie life is good. For everyone else it's panic and death. At each crime scene no DNA was discovered, no hair or fibers from Ronnie's clothing. He is still on the loose looking for more victims— he could be coming to a town near you, so lock your doors. Always look behind you. Beware. Scarecrow.

Serial Killer

Part 2

For two more years Dixie stayed with Merle. The abuse got worse, if you can imagine things getting worse. On a moonlit night Dixie stepped outside to enjoy a cool breeze. Merle was passed out drunk as usual on the mattress. As Dixie stepped back inside, a board from the rotted-out wood for flooring gave way. Only a lantern was lit. After feeling something underneath her foot, she reached down and found a loaded .38 revolver and yes thirty-four thousand dollars in cash, small bills, mostly what Merle had stashed several years ago.

Dixie was livid, living in these conditions for years. First, she throws the lantern in Merle's lap and then unloads the gun into his chest. As she walks the two miles to the pavement, she never looks back but could see the flames behind her. She reaches the pavement and walks seven miles into the daylight hours. The soles on her shoes are so worn out she feels the road with every step, reaching a police station in a small town she hadn't seen in years.

Dixie tells the sheriff what she had done. The FBI was called in and drove to her so-called home. It was still smoldering. Merle's body was burnt to a crisp. The local sheriff tells the FBI of Dixie's life, and she is totally exonerated and put in the witness protection program, now going back to school to finish her nursing degree.

I cannot and will not tell you what state she is now living in with a new name and finally enjoying life again. Now for Ronnie, he is on the run from every law enforcement you can imagine, last seen in Marmet, West Virginia, sticking to the backroads. He sees a porch light on by the road. Kicking the door in, he rapes and kills a ninety-four-year-old woman. He then searches her home and finds $2,800 in cash, takes her car, and begins his search for another victim. I had a feeling Ronnie knew I was writing about him. How? I can't explain it. I just knew.

Three weeks later I hear what I thought was a razor knife cutting our screen in our bedroom. I raced to my office, picked up a loaded model '97 Winchester shotgun, twelve-gauge with three-inch magnum shells. As he opened the window I screamed at Sherry to lie down. He was reaching for her. First shot I blew his left arm off. Second shot hit him in the chest and blew Ronnie out the window where he lay lifeless and still. I emptied the shotgun into him. No charges were filed against me for he was inside our home. Thank you for reading.

Scarecrow

Shadows in the Dark

Josh and Amy met in 2010 in the ninth grade. It was love at first sight for both of them. Josh came from a rich family, and Amy was from the poor side of Kingsport, Tennessee. Josh's parents didn't think much of Amy because she didn't come from money. Josh argued with his parents on Amy's behalf.

Amy is five feet eleven inches tall and a stone-cold beauty. Josh was six feet tall, a quarterback at his high school, and could have had any girl he pleased, yet he loved Amy. After graduation in 2014, they married. Josh's parents had started warming up to her. As time went along, Josh took a job at a local bank in Kingsport. As a teller, he soon climbed the ropes and was promoted to vice president of the bank in less than two years. His parents helped them buy a modest home in Kingsport. A year later Josh was running the bank, overseeing all loans and making $150,000 a year.

Amy decided to go back to school and learn how to aid autistic children. Her love for this was amazing. She excelled, and the children loved her as she did them. They had no children. Amy was unable to get pregnant. Josh and Amy decide to buy a single-engine plane. Josh took flying lessons and became a spot-on pilot. On a sunny September day, they decide to fly to Gutlinberg, Tennessee, to spend a few days and see the sights. Josh had been there before with his parents when he was just a young boy. As the plane left the runway and headed over the Great Smoky Mountains, a light came on in their plane that said they were losing oil pressure. Both of them were scared to death.

Josh made an attempt to land the plane. There was nowhere to land. After ten minutes, the plane lost power and crashed into the

Smoky Mountains. Miraculously they both survived with scratches and cuts, a bad one on Amy's forehead that was bleeding after hitting the windshield. Josh had a first-aid kit and bandaged Amy's head the best he could. The plane ended up on its nose with both wings torn off. Fortunately, Josh had a 40 mm pistol in the plane loaded with one in the chamber and sixteen in the magazine.

Now they were utterly lost in the woods. A day earlier two convicts had escaped from a maximum security prison in Knoxville, Tennessee, both on murder charges. As Josh and Amy made their way through the woods, they keep hearing someone talking and someone walking through the woods as the brush from the trees was making a swishing noise. So they stopped to listen more closely, the noise and talking stopped as well.

Both escaped convicts attacked Amy from behind, threw her to the ground. Josh turned and shot them both until they were lying lifeless on the ground. A chopper appeared with a spotlight, looking for the convicts. A basket was lowered down to where Josh and Amy were standing. A sheriff's deputy was on board. They took Josh's weapon away from him and carried them both to safety. Josh got his weapon a day later and received a commendation from the governor of Tennessee.

This story I dedicated to a good friend.

Shark Piss

Anyhoot here we go. Last night I wasn't feeling well, which happens from time to time. So I loaded up with my gear, which includes a six-inch knife and swimming trunks. Five hours later I arrive in South Padre Island, pull up to the beach, put my trunks on, and swim out about fifty yards with my knife. You have to have a knife.

The first shark I see is too small, swam a little further out. A twenty-feet great white nudges me in the back. It's battle time. I stab him in the throat multiple times. Dead as a door nail he is, dragged him back to shore, took my syringe and pulled five gallons of piss from him, filleted him up for shark steaks, which was what we had today on our charcoal grill. They were great—tender, tender, tender mercy—okeydoke. The shark piss I use to shoot up anywhere on your body. I've found shooting with a fresh syringe in my eye works best. Gets in the bloodstream faster, feeling good tonight, Scarecrow—it's a cure-all.

The Light

For most of us owning a home is a wonderful an investment and pride in keeping it looking nice and knowing one day it will be ours. Sounds good, right? Well, it is until something goes wrong. Then it's our responsibility to fix it ourselves or call someone to do the job for us and pay them more money than it's usually worth.

In our kitchen we have two lights. One is over the bar. The other lights up the kitchen very well, which is the one I use all the time. It's a fluorescent, four feet light. A bulb blew, so I went and bought two new ones at ten dollars for two. You can't buy just one. Wonder why that is? Unknown to me. Anyhoot I took off the cover and proceeded to change the bulb while standing on a ladder. As I twisted the light out, a plastic prong fell to the floor. The light fits in. Not happy at all about this.

Back to Lowe's I go to see if they sell the prong, and they did, so I bought two for ten dollars. Now I'm set. I ask Sherry to help me. She's on a six-feet ladder and I'm on a footstool on the other end. As I wire the new prong in, everything looks good, so now ready to put the bulbs back in. As I twist the two-prong bulb in, another prong breaks on the other end. Pissed beyond belief.

Two days go by with very little light in the kitchen, not going to let it beat us. Sherry says, "Why don't we go and buy a new four-feet light?" I'm game. Back to Lowe's we go and pick one out at forty dollars. Finally I'm thinking success. Nope. The new light will not line up with the holes in the ceiling, all the while we're having to kill the power in the kitchen, working with flashlights.

My feet are killing me from the footstool. Out to my shop to get a drill and bit for new holes. Before drilling new holes while holding the new fixture and marking where the light will be, Sherry and I were passing a marker back and forth to make sure it would fit, still on ladders and a footstool, which was another joy of our lives to do. I wired it in finally. Put the new bulbs in. Put the new cover on. Now time to see if our diligence worked.

Sherry went to our bedroom where the breaker box is while I stood there holding my breath. As she rounded the corner back into the kitchen, I turned the light on, and it worked. Elated we both were.

My take on this disaster: Buy a new light to begin with.

Dedicated to my bride, Sherry Summers. We are a team at most things we do to our home, and Billy Summers, my cousin and best friend who happens to be a master electrician. For those of you who read this story, I thank you.

Steve "Scarecrow" Summers

The Return

As darkness falls, the stars take their place in a sky waiting to be unveiled. Standing tall are the Appalachian Mountains of West Virginia surrounded with fog and clouds. Trees covered with snow begin to thaw as the sunrise peaks and burns through the clouds. Spring approaches. Some trees and branches find their way to their final resting place on the ground beneath, once stood tall beginning to topple from the weight of the snow, now melting away to make way for a spring that is overdue. Ice that hangs from the edge of cliffs begin to melt, giving way to a new spring, overdue for many people, and new growth for plants and trees to sprout as the warmer temperatures are now on the horizon of 2015.

In late spring of this year we will make our return to West Virginia. It's been twenty-four years since Sherry has seen her birthplace and a very long five years for a place I once lived for fifteen years. My mom is our most important person to see, who now resides in Beckley. Also, Sherry's dad's gravesite in Matheny will be visited.

We have talked of this day for many years, the two of us visiting together, and now finally it will happen. Friends will be notified before our final date is set. So we may see friends we haven't seen in many years. We are excited beyond anyone's imagination to be going together. It's been a hard road for us both the last three years. Waiting is harder than anything for me, for I have no patience for and will never regain something I wasn't given. The waters that will flow from the ice I once drank as a small boy will be remembered as I embark on a journey to cross the creek where I once lived in Kopperston with my family; then we were all together. Pennies that

I have lost through the years will be placed on the railroad tracks to regain childhood memories and brought back to Texas with me. So many things to reflect on that has not faded from my mind. Our time approaches.

Through the Eyes of
a Shelter Dog

The days seemed like weeks after Rocket was killed and Bella, our pup, came up missing. I was lost. Didn't know what to do with myself. After a few weeks, I thought I'll just buy a lab pup from a breeder. I couldn't see paying two thousand dollars for a dog. I have the money to do so. Yet I wouldn't.

A few days later I was looking online at the Ellis County SPCA. I didn't see any dogs I wanted, and then I came across Cali, a solid white Great Pyrenees mix. That evening I showed her to Sherry. The following day on a Sunday, almost two weeks ago, we went and saw Cali. She was underweight and very skittish. Two days later we carried Coco, our chocolate lab, to see how they reacted with each other. It went pretty well. Coco is seven years old, and Cali is two and a half years old. I knew Cali needed a lot of attention and love. We adopted her and brought her home.

We carried Cali to the vet. She was eaten up with fleas and needed to be spayed. We were told at the SPCA Cali had been adopted before and brought back after having a litter of puppies. I didn't care. We wanted her. Off to the vet we go. Fleas are now gone. A day later I carried her back to be spayed. She came home yesterday after spending the night at the vets and is doing fine. The vet called today. She has an intestinal parasite. Her blood work came back. I went today and picked up her medication. Also she is now on Heartgard. Still adjusting to a loving home, which is all she'll ever know here with us. She and Coco are getting along as well as can be expected.

Time is a healer, and she needs plenty of that. If by chance you adopt a shelter dog, give them a chance. Show them love and take care of them as you would yourself!

Thank you for your time for all who reads this.

Steve "Scarecrow" Summers

To the Moon and Back

A little prelude before the story. For those of you who were among my friends about this time last year, you may recall our cat Casper was lying on our AC unit sound asleep, and as I saw her, I thought, "A bad choice for you." I went into our home and turned on the AC unit. I made my way back to see her reaction. She was gone. A few days later a NASA representative came knocking. Casper had landed on the space shuttle orbiting the moon. A few days later she was returned to us.

And now the story (from the earth to the moon). NASA made an offer I couldn't refuse, to carry Sherry and I on the next flight to the moon, 238,857 thousand miles from Earth. We will be flown down to Houston from Waxahachie airport on the seventeenth of April 2015 for training for Sherry.

For my absence for the last seven days, I was in Houston to ensure I was ready for such a rush. The training was fun for me. Speed is something we both love. Fast cars and drag racing has been a thing we've loved for years, and now to go faster than a bullet awaits us.

On April 19, 2015, on an early Sunday morning at 6:00 a.m., we board the shuttle with one astronaut and fly to the moon. Three walks on the moon will be provided, also dinner at Mac's diner, which is now open there. Music will be carried on board with us, so we can dance on the moon. We are anticipating a glorious time while away, returning on April 30, 2015.

Happy trails to you. We hope to see you again.

Trains and Banks

Five men rode across the Missouri plains in the dark in a heavy fog, with the rain pouring down. The March winds were cutting them into as they rode. As the rain ceased and the wind calmed down, they settled in for the night in a clearing. Horses were unsaddled and fed, building a small fire to make some coffee for themselves with beans and jerky.

The year was 1875, and these men were not looking for anything but another place to rob. They were outlaws with the Pinkerton men of law on their trail. The morning sun arose. Then it was time to find a train that ran through close to where they had camped, and they knew where. As the train came rolling down the tracks, dynamite was used to blow the tracks as the train crossed them, killing the engineer with passengers on the train, as well as the second car that held the gold. They shot and killed three men guarding the gold and rode away with five thousand dollars' worth of gold to be sold in southern Missouri.

Nothing was ever enough for these five. They circled back now heading to Kansas, stopping in a one-horse town for a drink and supplies. Bounty signs were everywhere for their capture, dead or alive. No one stood up to draw on them. Lucky they didn't. Next morning drew fresh riding horses from the stable, carried their supplies and put them in their saddle bags, and rode off not killing anyone. A three-day ride to Kansas, rode into a populated town and robbed a bank. As they came out, one was hit in the shoulder, still managed to flip a kid standing on a rotted-out wooden floor in front of the bank a twenty-dollar gold piece.

A posse was formed to track them down, never to be found, made off this time with ten thousand in cash and seven thousand in gold. Having to stop to fix his wound, bleeding heavily, a six-inch knife was used to cut out the bullet and then cauterized the hole, camping for the night. Headed for Denver the next morning. Denver would be their demise. The Pinkertons, local law enforcement, was waiting. Telegraphs were common by this day and age.

It was too quite in Denver, and they were smart enough to know this, no one on the streets. As they turned back to ride away, three were shot in the back and killed, two wounded and hung two weeks later. People came from as far as a one hundred miles away to see the other two swing. Outlaws usually get their due, and these five did.

For all who may read this story, I thank you.

Steve "Scarecrow" Summers

Voices

The wind blows in northern Seattle, Washington. It's cold on November 23, 1997, as Brittany McCoy, at sixteen years old, walks along on a bridge at 1:00 a.m. She's looking down at the dark water that is flowing beneath wondering when it will reach its final destination.

For her, nothing has changed much in eight years. The voices she hears will not stop. She wonders why and cannot explain this to anyone. After many trips to see a psychiatrist, she is isolated and alone. An emptiness reigns within her.

At 7:00 a.m. her mom and dad go to wake her for school. She is not there. The police are called to find Brittany. She is found two days later in a park in Oregon with no idea how she got there. She covers her ears as two policemen approach her, trying so very hard to block out any sounds. As usual it doesn't help. She's in turmoil. On a bus back to Seattle to face her parents and what few friends she has, they stop.

The voices have disappeared for seven days. On November 30 she returns to hearing them all over again. She is frantic. Anxiety medication is prescribed by her psychiatrist with no results to be found. She is now eighteen years old. The voices continue. Finally she sits down with her mom and asks, "Why am I like this?"

Her mom hesitates, crying, and begins telling her of her great-grandmother Elizabeth. She tells her there is a history behind what has been happening to her for years. She listens like she has never listened to anyone before.

"The voices you hear are from Elizabeth."

In awe Brittany is without words, sits and wonders how someone who has passed away eighty-six years earlier could be talking to her. Mom sighs and says, "I have no idea other than she is leading down a road very few will ever travel, and if you will listen instead of trying to block her out, it will change your life forever." She agrees.

In 2001 they stop completely. Elizabeth has led Brittany to where she is perfectly happy, enrolls in school for criminal behavior science, and becomes the very best agent Seattle has to offer. In 2010 she is offered a job with the CIA. She takes the position and travels the world seeking out terrorists and evil that could and would harm this country and other countries as well. She is titled a ghost with the CIA. She only reports her findings to one person, her only contact, the director of the CIA.

You will never find her no matter how hard or long you look. Brittany is invisible to all who crosses her path. You may pass her anywhere and would think she is just another person who you don't know. She remains doing her job in a way that is perfect for many on this earth that are alive today because she cares and has left a lasting impression she has made on myself and others, to come soon saving lives. She is out there today on May 1, 2019.

Thank y'all for reading.

Steve "Scarecrow" Summers

Waiting on a Train

As the sun crests over the south Philly skyline, Diane's alarm clock goes off. It's 7:00 a.m. Time to get ready for work as she's done for the past thirty years.

Overnight a blizzard had blown in, dumping eighteen inches of snow. As she looks out her and Ed's apartment window, a disgusted look at what she sees. Ed had been fired from his job for drinking while there and never looked to find another. Now everything was on Diane's shoulders to keep a roof over their head and what little food she could buy on a teller's salary.

Ready now for another day, she walks down five flights of stairs. The elevator has been broken for years, and the landlord has no intention of having it repaired. After walking a block to catch her bus on a six-degree morning, she is half frozen from the north wind hitting her in the face at twenty-five miles an hour. The bus is an hour late arriving because of the snow.

Finally she boards the bus. Her feet hands and face are frozen. She has no gloves. Working for a small bank as a teller and she knows that's all she'll ever be, a small wage for a college graduate. That is where she and Ed met thirty-four years ago, fell in love and married. Their first ten years of marriage was good before Ed started drinking. First, he started verbal abuse; then a few years later, Diane would show up at work with bruises, a black eye from his backhand, kicked in the back as she would be lying on the floor. They had no children. Diane wanted at least two in the beginning. Now too far in years to consider having any children even if she found someone who truly loved her and treat her as she needed all these years.

Still a very attractive woman. She knew deep down she should have left him years ago, yet she stayed thinking things would get better. They never did for Diane. As winter passed on and spring was arriving, she gathered what little she had and packed a suitcase and left, no idea where she was going, but she was going. No family, brothers or sisters, her parents had passed on.

Diane bought a ticket at the train station for Tucson, Arizona. As she boarded she never looked back, found a job at a law firm in Tucson and is now practicing law, making the kind of money she deserves. Her degree from college was in law to begin with. She changed her name to Kim Miller, met a man who worships the ground she walks on. They will be married when Kim is sure he is the one.

For all who read the story, this kind of abuse is worldwide and will continue for all the women who stay with someone like Ed. Thank you for your time.

Steve "Scarecrow" Summers

Wheelchair

On October 27, 2017, pausing waiting on an a moment to pass, honestly I have dreaded this story for a very long time. I was going to write it. Then I wasn't. Looks like I am.

I left our home and traveled about a mile to buy gas. A perfect day sun was out warm for October as I left the convenience store and proceeded onto Highway 77 heading south toward Waxahachie. Out of nowhere an SUV pulled out in front of me. I was only running forty-five miles per hour when I hit it. The SUV rolled. No one was hurt in the SUV. Both my airbags deployed, burning my arms and hands. I thought I was fine.

As I stepped out of the truck, my left leg gave way. A policeman caught me and sat me back in my truck until paramedics arrived. I was rushed to Baylor-Scott White hospital in Waxahachie. Sherry was the first at the hospital, scared to death, and a friend of ours came as well. I was seen by a doctor. X-rays were done. They determined my left leg was fractured from the impact of the wreck. I was seen by an orthopedic surgeon two days later. He told Sherry and I that the impact had shattered my tibia and broke two bones in my knee. He said it was like you taking your fist and hitting the palm of your other hand as hard as you can, felt like this to me. He lets me come home, no surgery, just waiting to heal.

The days seemed like months. The two weeks Sherry stayed home with me I couldn't do anything on my own. My leg swelled to twice its normal size and stayed that way for two months. Finally the swelling receded little by little. Sherry bathed me, brought food. Nothing was left to be done. I've always loved her, but now it's a love that is unbreakable. My appetite was gone. Music I cared nothing anymore. Seemed most of anything I liked before was now a memory, except Sherry.

Now I'm getting better. A few things I once liked are coming back slowly. Sherry came home this morning with a walker. My heart shuttered when I saw the box on the floor. My first thought was "I'm not ready." I have learned to bathe myself, get my own food. Pretty much everything I once could I can now do in the wheelchair. My doctor says I'm ready. So tomorrow I will try. I don't feel ready. Sherry said we'll try tomorrow. Dreading tomorrow, afraid of falling and breaking it all over again.

I guess I don't sound like much of a man to anyone. There will be a small update on this story when I can walk on my own. Thank you. Steve "Scarecrow" Summers. Dedicated to my wife, Sherry Summers.

Wind

In the fall of 1957, off the coast of New England three brothers boarded their fishing boat at 5:00 a.m.—William, John, and Henry Rhea—so young to have the responsibility of keeping their large family fed. Their dad, William Senior, had passed one year earlier of a heart attack. William, the oldest, was eighteen, John was fifteen, Henry only thirteen years old, leaving behind their mother, Clara, and three sisters—Alyce, Jane, and Brittany.

As they started out, the ocean was calm and gentle. The boat was leaving a good trail. They could see the algae float to the top of the water. Henry, this being his first time out, was impressed as he sat and watched. Using only a compass to guide them, they soon were seventy-five miles out. William stopped the boat and set anchor then said, "It's time to go to work, brothers," using only a hand-cranked winch to lower the net thirty-five feet into the beautiful blue water. After two hours, all three were taking turns cranking the winch from the water. Sweating in the cold, finally reaching the side of the boat, they could see William had chosen a good spot. All smiles as they got their catch to where they could then swing into the lower galley.

They had caught crab and shrimp, packing them down with ice. Soon they would rest and eat. Sleep waits for dawn on Saturday morning, October 30, 1957. Instead they stayed up half the night telling tall tales and enjoying each other's company, as brothers usually do. As dawn broke, they were awakened by thunder and lightning. All three were scared yet never showed it. William started up the boat with a two-cycle forty-horsepower engine, headed away from what he saw on the horizon. After seven miles, as close as he could figure, he stopped, set anchor, again lowered the net into the water, now waves crashing into their boat.

John spoke up, "William, we can't wait this out." William knew John was right to stay. He knew they needed at least one more catch before they headed inland. Their small boat was beginning to rock. Water was rushing into the galley. They had no pump of any kind to help pull out the water. Seven hours later, night was falling soon. John and Henry said, "Cut the cable, let's go now."

William was not leaving the catch behind. Only one catch would not be enough to feed his sisters, mother, until the spring of 1958. William was now in a do-or-die situation. He screamed, "We can make it." The wind was now reaching seventy to eighty miles an hour. Henry was crying, thinking he was going to lose his own life along with his brothers as well. William started cranking as hard as humanly possible. The winch collapsed, hitting John in the head, bleeding, unconscious. William scrambled to check on him. His pulse was faint.

After twenty-seven hours, they reached shore. Their boat could be fixed, yet John was dead on arrival. For years to come William was never the same. He became an alcoholic, drifter, never once to returning to New England. He died of liver cirrhosis at the age thirty-two. The family survived, not knowing of William's demise. Henry held his family together for years to come, providing food. Shelter helped raise his sisters as their mother passed of a broken heart in 1963. The end.

Thank y'all for reading. Steve "Scarecrow" Summers.

Winds of Change

In the spring of 1929, a silent calm came across a small town in western Kansas. Many people were outside to witness all the beauty nature has to offer until the early morning hours of May 11, a community of only 632 people where everyone knew each other, good friends, neighbors far and wide across the thousands of acres of farmland, a small general store, one church. The roads were dirt. Well water was pumped daily for drinking water for the people of Ilene, a place where many worked seven days a week tending to their crops. On a Friday, May 13, storm clouds were forming from all directions. As the day progressed, the rain began to fall, a very happy sight for many.

As the roads became mud and crops filled with water, farmers and what few ranchers that lived close by were very happy. The general store closed down at precisely 6:00 p.m. daily and reopened at 6:00 a.m. The wind picked up to forty-five miles an hour, which was helping dry up the roads somewhat. No one owned a car or truck. Horses and mules were the way of transportation. Very few had wagons in Ilene. People were poor and scratched out what few things they owned.

Large families were the key to working in the fields. Some had as many as fourteen children who worked alongside their dads, at the early age of six years old girls and boys with blisters on their feet hands, while moms spent their day handwashing their clothes on a washboard, hanging them on a clothesline, nursing little ones from her own breast. Very few things were eaten they didn't grow themselves.

At Thanksgiving a turkey was traded for fresh eggs and canned goods at the general store. When Christmas came, handmade quilts was good enough for any house with dirt floors. Most were only two rooms to provide shelter from the cold winter months with only a fireplace to warm them. Life was very hard for all of Ilene. At 3:00 a.m. in the spring of 1929, a roar was heard from miles away. Everyone was awakened. Dads and moms knew what was coming, a tornado of complete destruction as the wind rose to over three hundred miles an hour. Crops were destroyed. Houses were flattened. Gone were the children, moms and dads, the general store. The church was the only standing structure left unharmed from this F5 tornado.

One survivor, Pastor Dale Owens, was found holding a wooden cross twice his size by the altar praying for the whole town out loud a day later by a sheriff from another town close by that wasn't touched by this horrific storm. Pastor Dale left Ilene and never looked back with tears flowing from his eyes, knowing all too well there was nothing or no one left alive. He rode double with the sheriff into another small town of 342 people who had no pastor or church. The town of Little Creek built a church, working side by side with Dale with only lumber, nails, rope block and pulley to erect a new home for Pastor Dale. He lived in the basement below.

From that day forward, everyone in Little Creek would crowd themselves in the large basement that was hand dug, lined with timbers to keep it stable. A local saw mill donated the massive timbers to make it where it still stands today, this October 13, 2019. On Sundays people would come from miles around to hear the words of wisdom Dale would preach, an educated man of the Bible. The cross that was left in Ilene was brought to Little Creek a woodworker carved in loving memory of the families of Ilene, pulled to the top of the church.

When people passed by the church, they would remove their hats in respect for all who lost their lives on that awful day when they heard the winds of change coming in their direction. The end.

I have seen up close what a tornado of this magnitude leaves in its wake. It is something you'd think is not possible, yet it is. I lived in Texas for most of my life. I'll never call another state home. Thank y'all for reading. Steve Summers. I dedicate this story to my mom, now eighty-nine years young, born in Lynch, Kentucky, as I was. I've seen her cry on Sunday mornings trying to get us up and ready for church. She only had a few skirts and blouses for herself to wear. Dad was the very same way with only one suit he proudly wore on Sunday mornings. They scarified all so we could have much more than they ever had in the days gone by. Also dedicated to Juanita Cook Barber who played a part of my life being changed when I was a freshman at Oceana High School in 1972.

Am I a good Christian? No, I sin each and every day. The only perfect Christian I know is Jesus. I said a few months ago my Facebook was now unplugged from what I post. It will stay this way until God calls me home. I have no apologies to anyone for what I post. I've never asked for anyone to agree on what I see and say. It is up to your discretion to live your life as you please.

CPSIA information can be obtained
at www.ICGtesting.com
Printed in the USA
BVHW031343160120
569727BV00001B/63

9 781796 076486